Absolute Essentials of Creative Thinking and Problem Solving

This concise textbook provides a comprehensive and clear overview of the theory and practice of creative problem solving from a management perspective.

The book works step by step through the creative thinking process. Beginning with theoretical frameworks, it considers ways of thinking, defining problems and structuring responses to them, techniques for generating ideas, evaluating and defining them, and finally how technology can be used within the creative problem solving process. Pedagogical features to aid learning include objectives at the start of each chapter, further reading suggestions, and practical examples.

Divided into ten short chapters to suit content delivery, this textbook is designed as either core or recommended reading for advanced undergraduate, postgraduate, MBA, and Executive Education students studying Creativity and Innovation, Management and Leadership, and Management Skills.

Tony Proctor is Emeritus Professor of Marketing at University of Chester, UK.

'A comprehensive reference book that's essential reading for anyone hoping to understand and develop better creative thinking and problem-solving skills.'

Absolute Essentials of Business and Economics

Textbooks are an extraordinarily useful tool for students and teachers, as is demonstrated by their continued use in the classroom and online. Successful textbooks run into multiple editions, and in endeavouring to keep up with developments in the field, it can be difficult to avoid increasing length and complexity.

This series of shortform textbooks offers a range of books which zero-in on the absolute essentials. In focusing on only the core elements of each sub-discipline, the books provide a useful alternative or supplement to traditional textbooks.

Titles in this series include:

Absolute Essentials of Project Management
Paul Roberts

Absolute Essentials of Business Behavioural Ethics
Nina Seppala

Absolute Essentials of Corporate Governance
Stephen Bloomfield

Absolute Essentials of Business Ethics
Peter A. Stanwick & Sarah D. Stanwick

Absolute Essentials of Creative Thinking and Problem Solving
Tony Proctor

For more information about this series, please visit: www.routledge.com/ Absolute-Essentials-of-Business-and-Economics/book-series/ABSOLUTE

Absolute Essentials of Creative Thinking and Problem Solving

Tony Proctor

Routledge
Taylor & Francis Group

LONDON AND NEW YORK

First published 2021
by Routledge
2 Park Square, Milton Park, Abingdon, Oxon OX14 4RN

and by Routledge
605 Third Avenue, New York, NY 10158

Routledge is an imprint of the Taylor & Francis Group, an informa business

British Library Cataloguing-in-Publication Data
A catalogue record for this book is available from the British Library

Library of Congress Cataloging-in-Publication Data
Names: Proctor, Tony, author.
Title: Absolute essentials of creative thinking and problem solving / Tony Proctor.
Description: New York: Routledge, 2021. | Series: Absolute essentials of
business and management | Includes bibliographical references and index.
Identifiers: LCCN 2020056110 (print) | LCCN 2020056111 (ebook) |
ISBN 9780367643454 (hardback) | ISBN 9781003124054 (ebook)
Subjects: LCSH: Problem solving. | Creative thinking. |
Management–Technological innovations.
Classification: LCC HD30.29 .P7626 2021 (print) |
LCC HD30.29 (ebook) | DDC 658.4/03–dc23
LC record available at https://lccn.loc.gov/2020056110
LC ebook record available at https://lccn.loc.gov/2020056111

ISBN: 978-0-367-64345-4 (hbk)
ISBN: 978-0-367-64346-1 (pbk)
ISBN: 978-1-003-12405-4 (ebk)

Typeset in Times New Roman
by Deanta Global Publishing Services, Chennai, India

Contents

Introduction

This is a very short introduction to creative thinking and problem solving. It is comprehensive in nature and provides pointers to key aspects of the subject. You will be provided with an overview of important aspects of creative thinking and problem solving. To make the subject matter clearer and readily understandable, the subject has to be presented in a logical and structured manner. The pedagogical features of the book include essential summaries, focused references/readings, and online supplements to help achieve this objective.

There are many definitions of creativity, but in business it refers to finding insights into problems. Any person seeking to further the interests of their organisation needs to be able to think creatively. As we move towards the third decade of the current century this need has become an urgent necessity among businesses in the developed world. It not surprising that interest in creative problem solving has continued to be high. In a world that is constantly changing and presenting new challenges, pathways to the solution of new kinds of problems are always in demand. Nothing is certain and even long-established businesses can begin to crumble in a matter of months, so radical new ways of looking at problems seem to be very much the order of the day. However, creative thinking should not be seen as the 'universal antidote' capable of curing all, but it offers ways of examining problems that force us to questions fundamental issues. It makes us challenge basic assumptions. There are no such things as firm foundations – the bedrocks of civilisation can crumble into dust while we look on in awe and trepidation!

The book is designed specifically for those who want a quick overview of the subject matter. It will appeal to students at all levels. Its concise nature means that you can read it anywhere at any time and it will be especially good for those who need to revise material or who just want to check up on some key point about the subject. Throughout the book there are ample illustrations of the key points.

Tony Proctor, Chester, 2021

1   Theoretical frameworks

Introduction

First, we look at definitions of creative thinking and move on to consider theories regarding its nature. We consider the brain as a processor of information, where creativity is explained best by the neuro-physiological functioning of the brain, as the most appropriate of these theories. Whole-brain and two-brain theories exemplify this latter approach. We shall see a connection between the neuro-physiological functioning of the brain and the cognitive theory of creative problem solving discussed later in the chapter. We finish the chapter by examining ideas about analogical reasoning. The theoretical issues raised in this chapter act as a background for appreciating the elements of the next chapter, which introduces the creative problem solving process.

What is creative thinking?

Wertheimer (1945) suggested that creative thinking involved breaking down and restructuring our knowledge in order to gain new insights into its nature. Creativity is something which occurs when we are able to organise our thoughts in such a way that readily leads to a different and even better understanding of the situation we are considering.

Rickards (1988: 225) advocated a view of creativity as an 'escape from mental stuckness.' Sternberg and Lubart (1995) argue that creativity requires a coming together of six clear-cut yet interconnected assets: intellectual abilities, knowledge, styles of thinking, personality, motivation, and environment. However, Simonton (2017) points out that there is no dearth of alternative definitions of creativity. These various definitions seem to agree that creativity involves an ability to come up with new, different, and even useful viewpoints. However, any definition of creativity is complicated because the concept is multi-faceted. Let us now turn to consider how creativity is thought to be generated.

Early theories of creative thinking

There are a number of schools of thought as to the origin of creativity (Henry, 1991): grace, accident, association, cognitive, personality.

Grace

Creativity is something of a mystery, drawing forth images of wonderful insights, imaginative efforts, illumination, and intuitions that come from nowhere. It seems the work of magic. The idea of genius may add force to this notion since creative artists, musicians, etc. seemed to be endowed with superhuman potential. Creativity, in this sense, is seen as a divine gift.

Accident

This is the opposite of it being a divine gift. It rises by chance. Holders of this view offer various types of accidental discoveries such as those of immunisation arising from an interruption in work, radioactivity from the wrong hypothesis, and the smallpox vaccination from observation.

Association

This is the most popular and suggests that applying procedures from one area to another gives rise to novel associations, and that such associations form the bedrock of creative ideas. The notion was popularised by Koestler (1964) under the term 'bisociation,' and it underlies the justification for many divergent thinking techniques, such as lateral thinking and brainstorming.

Cognitive

Creativity is a normal human activity. It uses cognitive processes like recognition, reasoning, and understanding. Many inventors work at a problem for years. Research has concluded that ten years of intense preparation is needed for significant creative contributions. Deep thinking about an area over a long period leaves the discoverer informed enough to notice anomalies that might be significant. Highly creative people are strongly motivated and seem able to concentrate over a long period.

Personality

Creativity is a state of mind which can be learnt. Some people seem to have a facility for it while others do not, but they can improve with practice.

Mental barriers to creativity have to be removed to allow innate spontaneity to flourish. Creative acts are not isolated acts of perception, they require an emotional disposition, too, for any new idea replaces and in effect destroys the previous order. It takes courage and persistence to brave the resistance that any change seems to engender.

The five perspectives make some valid points, but here we pay particular credence to the cognitive theory.

The brain as an information processor

Ideas are a form of information and as such are formulated in the brain. The brain has two cerebral hemispheres – a left and a right. The primary mental processes of these hemispheres include vision, hearing, body senses, reasoning, language, and non-verbal visualisation. Within each hemisphere is to be found one half of the limbic system. This is a control centre that governs such things as hunger, thirst, sleeping, waking, body temperature, heart rate, blood pressure, and emotions. The limbic system plays an important role in transferring incoming information into memory. The two cerebral hemispheres and the two halves of the limbic system make up the four quadrants of the brain. The upper quadrants represent the cerebral hemispheres, while the lower quadrants represent the two halves of the limbic system.

Fibres connect the two cerebral hemispheres, and these fibres carry communications both within and between the two hemispheres. When solving complex problems or other intricate work, different thinking methods are required. The brain switches signals back and forth very rapidly between different areas within the two hemispheres via the fibre links. Switching thinking modes within the cerebral hemispheres (within each of the two upper quadrants) is simple, but switching between the two lower or upper quadrants is more difficult. Diagonal switching is most difficult because there are no fibre connections between diagonally opposite quadrants of the brain.

The Whole Brain/Four-Quadrant Model

Herrmann (1990) showed that it is possible to build a model of the human brain with two paired structures, the two halves of the cerebral system and the two halves of the limbic system. This permits one to differentiate between not only the more popular notions of left/right brain, but also the more sophisticated notions of cognitive/intellectual which describe the cerebral preference, and visceral, structured, and emotional which describe the limbic preference.

Herrmann's Whole Brain Model also made use of the concept of dominance. Evidence indicates that, wherever there are two of anything in the body, one of them is naturally dominant over the other. For example, we may be right- or left-handed. We can also be thought of as predominantly right- or left- 'brained.' The implications of this for the way in which we prefer to do things are important. Indeed, sometimes our preferred way of doing things may well be counterproductive. Predominantly left-brained thinkers may experience more difficult relationships with colleagues than right-brained thinkers because they are not as sensitised to other people. On the other hand, it may be that predominantly right-brained thinkers need to have goals and a schedule set for them to help them be more efficient.

The Whole Brain Model (Figure 1.1) presents four distinct thinking styles:

1 The upper (cerebral) left

A – analytical, mathematical, technical, and problem solving

2 The lower (limbic) left

B – controlled, conservative, planned, organised, and administrative in nature

3 The lower (limbic) right

C – interpersonal, emotional, musical, and spiritual

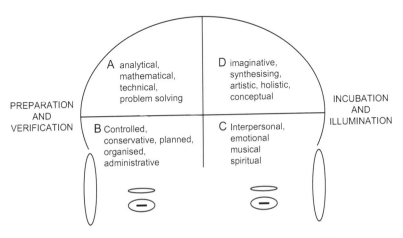

Figure 1.1 Brain theories – the Whole Brain Model (Hermann/Wallis)

   4   Upper (cerebral) right

D   – imaginative, synthesising, artistic, holistic, and conceptual modes

Among other things:

- Predominantly A-quadrant thinkers prefer organising information logically in a framework, listening to lectures and reading textbooks, studying example problems and solutions, thinking through ideas, doing scientific/academic research, judging ideas based on facts, criteria, and logical reasoning, dealing with reality and current problems
- Predominantly B-quadrant thinkers like finding practical uses for knowledge learnt, planning projects, practising new skills, writing practical guides about how to do something
- Predominantly C-quadrant thinkers like to be very organised and precise in their work
- Predominantly D-quadrant thinkers like to take an overall view of new topics (not the detail), to take the initiative, ponder on possible outcomes of actions, use visual aids, solve open-ended problems, enjoy wild ideas, experiment, rely on intuition rather than on logic, synthesise ideas, approach a problem from different angles

From the point of view of undertaking creative problem solving activities, type-D thinkers seem to have the most favourable frame of mind for this activity.

During the 1960s, research on the brain caused scientists to conclude that both hemispheres are involved in higher cognitive functioning. It was found that each half of the brain produced different modes of complex thinking. The main argument to develop was that there appear to be two modes of thinking – verbal and non-verbal – which tended to be conducted separately by the left and right hemispheres, respectively. This in turn led initially to a number of 'brain'-related theories concerning creative thinking, notable amongst which was Roger Sperry's Left Brain/Right Brain Theory. According to this theory, the left brain is used for logical thinking, judgement, and mathematical reasoning, while the right brain is the source of dreaming, feeling, visualisation, and intuition.

Convergent and divergent thinking

Guilford (1967) claimed and cited evidence to support the view that divergent thinking processes, as opposed to convergent thinking processes, are related to creativity. Divergent thinking involves a broad search for decision options with respect to a problem for which there is no unique answer. In the divergent processes, the generation of alternatives involves finding many combinations of elements that may provide many possible answers. Fluency of thinking and originality characterise a divergent search for alternatives, rather than a rigorous adherence to prescribed steps and criteria for finding some uniquely 'correct' result. In a convergent search, the opposite is true; that is, it is a unique solution to meet the prescribed criteria that are sought. As Guilford (1975) points out, however, these two modes are not necessarily used in isolation and can be intermixed in so far as a divergent approach can be used on the way to a convergent solution. The extent to which the whole process can be characterised as divergent or convergent is relative rather than absolute and depends on the degree of limitations imposed on the answer. We might thus conclude that both divergent and convergent thinking contribute to the gaining of creative insights.

Guilford, as discussed by Dacey (1989), argues that a major impediment to effective convergent thinking lies not in the use of a problem solving paradigm but in the selection of a good one. Dacey (ibid.) has referred to Edward de Bono's theories of divergent thinking which combine vertical and lateral dimensions. De Bono states, 'vertical thinking digs the same hole deeper; lateral thinking is concerned with digging a hole in another place' (Dacey, ibid.). Seemingly, if that hole is in the wrong place, no amount of logic is going to put it in the right place. Therefore, although the Creative Problem Solving Method (CPSM) requires these dual thought processes, the model will not be constructive unless the 'digger' is on the right track.

It is argued that the function of divergent thinking is to 'broaden out' the thought process and thus reject blinkered thinking and disregard constraints on problem solving. Convergent thinking applies a greater degree of judgement and narrow focus. The argument is, however, the subject of some criticism. Weisberg (1986) considers that divergent thinking is not in fact an important aspect of creativity and studies have shown that creative ability is not related to divergent thinking ability. He argues that novel solutions to problems can in fact be achieved without it. He feels that creative problem solving does always require a fresh perspective.

The cognitive theory of creativity

Here we will look at how information is thought to be stored and retrieved from memory. In the next chapter we will look at how it might be retrieved in a manner which enables ideas to be generated and problems to be tackled.

Cognitive processes have been a much-disputed topic for many years. Various schools of psychology – the psychoanalytical, gestalt, and associative – all have their various perspectives on the subject. At the core of the thinking process is memory. It is thought that there may be both long-term and short-term memory. Short-term memory can hold only a small amount of information at any one time. Long-term memory, on the other hand, has a vast information-storage capacity. If we paid attention to all the things our senses are reporting at any particular moment and took them all into consideration, it would be very hard for us to make decisions. We can only hold a few items in our short-term memory, and that is what enables us to focus on what is important and to act quickly.

Long-term memory may be thought of as being filled with all the images, sounds, odours, and other types of sensory data in an assembled form and which we hold as a symbolic picture of our remembered information. Information itself is learnt from our experience and stored in chunks along with cues associated with the information.

We can often recall the wanted material by recalling the unwanted accompaniment. The learnt material and the cues form complex networks of information. Thus, when we are trying to think of objects that might resemble 'red faces' we might find it easier not to concentrate our minds upon 'faces' but rather to make connections with similar images – beetroot, the setting sun, etc. From a creativity point of view, it is how we make the connections along and across the networks that is of interest.

According to McClelland (1981), information about people, events, and objects is stored in several interconnected units rather than in a single location. The strength of the connections between these units increases as a result of learning. Subsequent retrieval of information about a particular person, event, or object involves gaining access to one or more of the relevant units, followed by a spread of activation to other relevant units. This provides an explanation for the fact that we seem to possess both episodic (or autobiographical) memories and semantic (or knowledge-based) memories. For example, we may possess information about several cars with which we are familiar, and we also have knowledge of the general concept of the car. Accordingly, the stimulus word 'car' leads to the activation of several units referring to specific cars, and an averaging process indicates the typical features of cars in general.

The process of thinking effectively means accessing very large volumes of information in long-term memory via a bottleneck memory space, which takes the form of short-term memory. While the speed of access to long-term memory is extremely rapid, it appears possible to consider only small amounts of information at a time. Bottlenecks are symptomatic of inefficient operation and usually result in a slowdown or cessation of operation if they become overloaded or choked. This view of the human information-processing system points to limitations in terms of its efficiency. In problem solving or trying to think creatively, we immediately come up against these limitations. Creative problem solving aids need to help us circumvent these difficulties if they are to be useful aids to thinking.

Not only is the efficiency of the human information-processing system constrained by its own structure; it is also affected by how people use it. It is thought that through a process of selective perception or filtering we pay attention to only certain features of things we sense. The concept of a perceptual filter is important because of the factors that constrain it – for instance, beliefs, attitudes, etc. Blinkered thinking may occur because of the various beliefs and attitudes we hold and the impact they have on our perceptual filter.

How knowledge is stored in memory

Understanding how knowledge is thought to be stored in human memory enables us to appreciate how long-term memory may be organised and how the search of long-term memory may be conducted. Among the earliest ideas on representation were those of Quillian (1968), who introduced the notion of the semantic network. This maintained that knowledge can be represented by a kind of directed, labelled graph structure in which the basic structural element is a set of interrelated nodes (Figure 1.2).

Semantic network theory has a place in the structure of representation, but it does not allow one to structure knowledge into higher-order representational units. Nevertheless, externalising this form of representation can be employed effectively in facilitating creative thinking.

Schemas

Schemas are learnt as a result of experience and reside in memory to be called upon at any time. Schemas are packets of information in which there is a fixed part, representing those characteristics which are always true of exemplars of the concept, and a variable part, which need not always be true. The schema for the concept of 'elephant' would contain constant parts such as 'elephant has a trunk' and variable parts such as 'elephant can be found in a zoo.' Variables have default values if the incoming information is unspecified. Thus, the concept of 'pensioner' might have as its fixed part 'is retired from his or her former occupation,' but unless the variable 'age' is specified this would default to 'old.' Schemas can also be embedded within one another so that a schema consists of a configuration of sub-schemas and so on.

Schemas influence the way that new information is processed. The schema that is currently activated guides the selection of what is to be encoded and

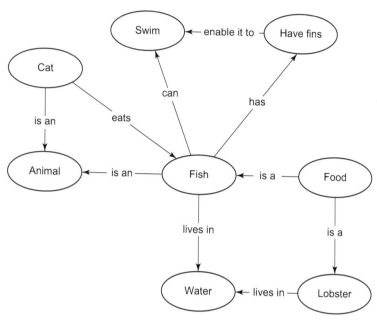

Figure 1.2 Semantic network

stored in memory, so that information relevant to that schema is more likely to be remembered than non-relevant information. The schema provides a framework within which the information can be stored and which can be used at retrieval to guide search processes.

Scripts, deltacts, and MOPS

Workers in the area of Artificial Intelligence made important contributions to cognitive science. This perspective suggests that we make use of special types of schemas known as scripts and deltacts (Schank and Abelson, 1977) in dealing with problems. Scripts allow people to make inferences about a situation and are assembled from smaller data elements called MOPS (memory organisation packets). MOPS serve to organise experiences around essential similarities, enabling people to recognise old situations in new guises and to draw conclusions.

Scripts are stereotyped responses based on experience. It is argued that, in trying to cope with a new situation or problem, people try to recall previous ways in which they have dealt with similar problems: they try to recall a script. A script is an organised memory structure that describes a suitable sequence of activities to deal with a particular problem or situation. Scripts guide what people do, think, and say. Retrieving an appropriate script from memory allows people to deal with a situation or a problem in an effective manner.

Schank and Abelson (1977) suggested that people undertake 'goal directed behaviour' to cope with problems or situations where a relevant script cannot be retrieved (i.e. because they have never learnt one in the first instance). Discovering the goal may be part of the process, and sometimes the goal may have to be implied from several aspects of a description. In addition, one has to find a set of ways in which to satisfy the main goal. These take the form of sub-goals and associated plans which Schank and Abelson (ibid.) termed 'deltacts.'

Schank and Abelson (ibid.) argued that higher-level structures, which they termed themes, serve as nuclei around which goals, plans, and scripts are organised. In trying to solve a problem it is suggested that we organise our thoughts around a theme. For example, imagine that the boss has decided to remove the opportunity of earning extra money from people working in an office. There are various possible responses that workers could make to this action, but one theme that could emerge is that of challenging the boss's authority to prevent people earning extra money. Scripts, deltacts, etc., would be organised around the theme of 'challenge authority,' and, as a consequence, solutions to emerge might be such things as 'appeal to a higher authority in the organisation' or even, if it were possible, 'flout the boss's authority.'

How we get ideas

Building on the concept of schemas, scripts, deltacts, and themes we can suggest how ideas may be generated and the role that creative problem solving aids can play in helping the ideas to emerge. It is supposed that we store all our information, knowledge, and experience in a huge 'mental book.' How we deal with a problem is influenced by our perceptions in relation to its content. Our perceived problem has features and attributes which constitute a particular pattern. We then search our memory for a matching pattern related to the subject of the problem (schema or script).

It may be that we do not find any relevant patterns in our memory which can match with those of the problem. Where this is the case, then creative problem solving aids can be extremely useful.

Pattern recognition

There are several theories of how we recognise patterns. In the context of creative thinking then template matching and prototype-matching seem to be the most appropriate theories to examine.

Template matching theory assumes every perceived object (schema, script, or MOP) is stored as a 'template' into long-term memory (Shugan, 2002). Incoming information is compared to these templates to find an exact match (Gregg, 2013). That is, all sensory input is compared to multiple representations of an object to produce a single conceptual understanding. The theory considers perception to be a recognition-based process. It assumes that everything we see, we understand only through past experience of it, which in turn then informs our future understanding of it.

In contrast, prototype-matching suggests incoming sensory input is compared to one average prototype. This point of view argues that exposure to a series of related stimuli produces a 'typical' prototype based on their shared features. There is then a reduction in the number of stored templates resulting from the standardisation of them into a single representation (Shugan, 2002). The prototype supports perceptual flexibility, because, unlike in template matching, it allows for variability in the recognition of novel stimuli and enables us to find an exact solution to the problem. This is either because we have previously successfully tackled and solved the same problem or because we have, at some time, learnt and stored information on how to solve this particular kind of problem.

Different individuals may exhibit a tendency towards one or the other of these two modes of pattern recognition. We might identify prototype-matching with individuals who have a tendency to be divergent thinkers.

The following illustrates the idea of prototype pattern matching.

Suppose we have chunks of information (scripts, schemas) which relate to different kinds of 'bottleneck' situations. Imagine, for example, that one refers specifically to watching the emptying of liquid from a bottle. In looking for patterns in the information we might consider the following features about the process:

Feature 1. There is a large volume of water to be poured from the bottle.
Feature 2. The bottle has a narrow outlet.
Feature 3. As we pour, water stops and start to flow as the volume builds up at the neck of the outlet.
Feature 4. The whole process of emptying out the water is slowed down by the narrow outlet.

Now let us turn to look at two other situations about which we have information and which appear to have similarities with that of 'pouring water out of a bottle':

1   Rush-hour traffic flow
    Feature 1. Large volume of traffic.

Feature 2. Limited carriageway capacity at certain points forcing traffic to slow down to avoid accidents.

Feature 3. Traffic stops and starts.

Feature 4. The speed and process of passage slowed down in comparison with other times of the day.

2 Hospital routine operations

Feature 1. Large number of new patients on waiting lists.

Feature 2. Treatment of patients impeded by lack of available beds, staffing shortages, and need to give preference to emergency operations.

Feature 3. Hold-ups and increased waiting times for patients.

Feature 4. Slow down speed with which treatment is delivered.

For each of the above situations we may know ways of dealing with the problems each of the situations presents and this may be extremely useful where we are dealing with new situations that are *directly* comparable with one or other of the above situations. In other words, they would be TEMPLATES for how to deal with the new situation. However, it might well be that while a new situation which has arisen may concern 'bottlenecks' it does not have a matching pattern (set of similar features or attributes) with any one of the above template patterns. This where the notion of the PROTOTYPE pattern, based on 'averaging' the features of the TEMPLATES, comes into play. In the example illustrated here the prototype pattern might be:

Prototype

Feature 1. Large volume/numbers flowing through a system.

Feature 2. Progress may be impeded by inadequacies in facilities at certain points of the process.

Feature 3. Flow subject to interruptions.

Feature 4. Progress is slower than desired/ expected.

Associated with the PROTOTYPE may be general ideas on how to deal with situations of this type. Trying to match the new situation with the PROTOTYPE may then enable insights into the new situation to be found. If these prove to be useful, then the new situation (and any insights gained) can become a TEMPLATE itself and in turn influence the nature of the PROTOTYPE on a future occasion. The process is summarised in Figure 1.3.

This approach to creative problem solving is mirrored in analogical thinking and the use of analogical reasoning techniques such as synectics. In the next chapter we will look at how the theoretical ideas in this chapter can be related to practice.

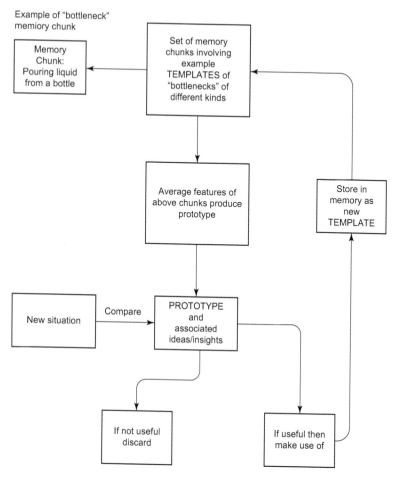

Example of "bottleneck" memiory chunk

Figure 1.3 Pattern matching using TEMPLATE and PROTOTYPE

Questions

1 'There are no theoretical underpinnings to the creative problem solving process.' Discuss.
2 Differentiate between divergent and convergent thinking. What role do both play in the creative problem solving process?
3 How would you explain the essence of the cognitive theory of creativity?
4 Explain the relevance of scripts, deltacts, and MOPs to how memory is stored and retrieved from memory.

5   Simonton (2017) points out that there is no dearth of alternative definitions of creativity. Why should this be the case?

References

Dacey, J.S. (1989) *Fundamentals of Creative Thinking*, Lexington, MA: Lexington Book.

Gregg, H. (2013) 'Perception and perceptual illusions', *Psychology Today*. Retrieved from https://www.psychologytoday.com/blog/theory-knowledge/201305/perception-and-perceptual-illusions

Guilford, J.P. (1967) *The Nature of Human Intelligence*, New York: McGraw-Hill.

Guilford, J.P. (1975) 'Creativity: a quarter century of progress', in I.A. Taylor and J.W. Getzels (eds), *Perspectives in Creativity*, Chicago, IL: Aldine. 37–59.

Henry, J. (1991) *The Creative Manager*, London: SAGE.

Herrmann, N. (1990) *The Creative Brain*, Lake Lure, NC: Brain Books.

Koestler, A. (1964) *The Act of Creation*, New York: Penguin Books.

McClelland, J.L. (1981) 'Retrieving general and specific information from stored knowledge of specifics', in *Proceedings of the Third Annual Meeting of the Cognitive Science Society*, 170–172.

Rickards, T. (1988) 'Creativity and innovation: a transatlantic perspective', in *Creativity and Innovation Year-Book*, Manchester: Manchester Business School.

Schank, R. and Abelson, R. (1977) *Scripts, Plans, Goals and Understanding: An Enquiry into Human Knowledge Structure*, Hillsdale, NJ: Lawrence Erlbaum.

Shugen, W. (2002) 'Framework of pattern recognition model based on the cognitive psychology', *Geo-spatial Information Science*, 5(2), 74–78.

Simonton, D.K. (2017) 'Big-C versus little-c creativity: definitions, implications, and inherent educational contradictions', in Beghetto, R. and Sriraman, B. (eds), *Creative Contradictions in Education. Creativity Theory and Action in Education*, vol 1. Cham, Springer. 3–19.

Sternberg, R.J. and Lubart, T.I. (1995) *Defying the Crowd*, New York: Free Press.

Weisberg, R.W. (1986) *Creativity, Genius and Other Myths*, New York: W. H. Freeman.

Wertheimer, M. (1945) *Productive Thinking*, New York: Harper & Row.

Further reading

Amabile, T.M. (2013) 'Componential theory of creativity', In Kessler, E.H. (ed.), *Encyclopedia of Management Theory*, SAGE, London, 134–139.

Hong, T.S. and Proctor, T. (2015) 'Exploration of a creative problem solving technique', in Sidin, S. and Marai, A. (eds), *Proceedings of the Academy World Marketing Congress Developments in Marketing Science*. Kuala Lumpur

Olteţeanu, Ana-Maria (2015) "Seeing as' and Re-representation: their relation to insight, creative problem-solving and types of creativity', in Besold,

T., Kühnberger, K.-U., Schorlemmer, M. and Smaill, A., *Proceedings of the Workshop 'Computational Creativity, Concept Invention, and General Intelligence'*, Osnabrüc, Publications of the Institute of Cognitive Science, vol. 02-2015.

Proctor, T. (1996) 'Paradigm shift: a new perspective involving analogical thinking', *Management Decision*, 34(7), 33–38.

Runco, M.A. (2010) 'Divergent thinking, creativity and ideation', in Kaufman, J.C. and Sternberg, R.J. (eds), *The Cambridge Handbook of Creativity*, Cambridge, UK: University Press, 413–446.

2 Blocks to creativity

Introduction

Creative thinking and problem solving do not necessarily come naturally to people. In the case of individuals, there are blocks to creative thinking and creative problem solving. The blocks are essentially of two varieties – individual and organisational. First, we examine the need to be ready for change and the need to deal with new kinds of problem. Then we turn our attention to the various personal blocks that people may encounter when trying to solve problems, think creatively, and deal with new kinds of problems. These blocks are to do with mindset and with factors to do with perception, emotion, expression, and cultural influences. The chapter then continues by discussing how these blocks can be diagnosed and overcome. We then move on to blocks encountered in teams and then the conditions under which creativity may be encouraged in organisations.

The need to be ready for change

Executives must be ready for anything which requires having the necessary tools to combat change proactively. If we were not at times 'blocked' in our thinking, we would not need creative problem solving methods. In this chapter we shall first consider the nature of problem solving within the information-processing paradigm before going on to examine *individual* and *organisational* blocks to creative thinking. In addition, we shall look at ways of dealing with both kinds of blocks. It is the existence of these blocks that gives rise to the need for a structured creative problem solving process and for training to help overcome particular mindsets.

Mindset

Mindset is a condition where an individual is over-sensitised to some part of the information available at the expense of other parts. Mindset can be useful:

- It helps us to become sensitised to some important things and serves us well – for example, red lights act as warnings and alert us to impending danger
- As a result of learning from experience, mindset sensitises us to patterns that remind us of ways which have enabled us to solve past problems. We do not have to reinvent the wheel each time we encounter the same problem. For example, if when dealing with an irate customer we have found an approach that seems to be satisfactory from the point of view of dealing with the situation, when we subsequently encounter another irate customer, we can deal with the situation using our acquired knowledge

When mindset blocks us

Luchins (1942) showed how mindset under certain circumstances can produce fixation and stereotyping in problem solving behaviour. The phenomenon may show itself under conditions where the individual has discovered a strategy that initially functions well in solving certain tasks but later blocks the realisation of new and simpler solutions to similar problems.

Duncker (1945) investigated how past experience may block productive problem solving. He suggested the expression 'functional fixedness' to refer to a block against using an object in a new way that is required to solve a problem. Interesting real-life examples of functional fixedness include the computer having been used for a long time as a calculator before its use as a general symbol manipulator was envisaged.

It would seem that, while mindset can provide us with substantial benefits, unfortunately, there are times when it can stand in the way of progress. Mindset can create difficulties for executives when they are facing new problems. When stuck on a problem, executives tend to follow their mindset, and this may be counterproductive as far as previously unencountered problems are concerned. Mindset is often characterised by one-right-answer thinking, always looking for reasons why something will not work and an over-regard for logical thinking.

Executives may have learned from past experience that a particular way of dealing with a problem usually leads to a satisfactory solution. Constant successful application of the approach reinforces the belief that this is the correct way to approach the problem, and even the *only* way to approach the problem. When a new problem arrives that defies solution by the learned approach, executives become stuck and do not know what to do.

Negative or 'yes, but' thinking arises out of executives' zeal to cater for contingencies. It is only natural that they should try to ensure that any project will stand a good chance of being successful, and good management practice advocates that executives should consider what may go wrong and make contingency plans. Every suggestion is therefore questioned and critiqued in order to make sure that the risk of failure is minimised. However, the process of criticism itself can stifle creativity by inducing a negative mindset. Constructive criticism is required. Rather than making the comment 'yes, but,' one should use the phrase 'yes, and.' For example, faced with the suggestion of making redundancies, the normal response might be: 'Yes, but that will only lead to unrest on the shop-floor and possible strike action.' The better response would be: 'Yes, and wouldn't it be useful, since we can then find other jobs for those people within the company.'

An over-regard for logical thinking can also create a barrier to creative thinking. Sometimes we have to take steps into the dark, as it were, based upon a hunch or upon intuition. We may have a feeling that what we are doing is the best course of action even though we cannot justify it in a traditionally logical way to ourselves. Perhaps the logical justification only becomes apparent *post facto* – we can see with hindsight that what we did was the right thing to do. Somehow, we cannot perceive beforehand the logical justification – we have a perceptual block. The notion of perceptual blocks is discussed later in the chapter.

Mindset may reflect perceptual, cultural, and emotional barriers (Arnold, 1962); intellectual and expressive blocks (Adams, 1974); mood (Shapiro *et al.*, 2000); state of happiness (Argyle, 2001). Mood, thinking, and even personality may all be interrelated (Russ, 1999).

Let us now turn to consider the factors that underpin mindset in more detail.

Personality

Personality appears to influence how people process information. In the past there have been concerted efforts to define dimensions of personality and to develop measurement tools to relate how people are influenced in processing information according to their predisposition on these dimensions. Building on investigations into the relevance of Jung's theory of individuals' preferences a number of personality types have been suggested. Arguably, most personality types should be able to think creatively. However, those identified as 'introverts,' 'thinking,' or 'judging' types may be less comfortable with thinking creatively. Introverts need time to think and clarify their ideas while individuals who have a 'thinking' preference try to use logic and analysis during problem solving. 'Judging' types prefer structure and organisation and will want the problem solving process to demonstrate closure.

Another way of looking at how personality influences ability to think creatively is encapsulated in the 'five-factor model' which identifies conscientiousness, agreeableness, neuroticism, openness to experience, and extraversion as relevant personality traits (King *et al.*, 1996). Ability to think creatively appears to be positively associated with openness to experience and negatively related to conscientiousness (. We might deduce from this that individuals who can think creatively make use of their openness to new ideas and experiences in the search for solutions. On the other hand, those deemed 'conscientious' often work within a restrictive set of rules that stymies their problem solving processes, thereby not allowing them to consider novel or unusual solutions.

Thinking style

Kirton (1976) suggested that people exhibit two broad creative thinking styles. These he labels 'adaptors' and 'innovators.' Adaptors like to take ideas and improve on them, preferring incremental innovation and doing things better rather than seeking to find the very best way of doing things. Innovators like to find new ideas by challenging and changing accepted ways of doing things. These different styles of thinking influence the way in which people approach a problem. In some circumstances, this would help to solve a problem but in others would prevent them from making progress towards a solution.

Learning styles

Learning styles present another perspective from which to understand how people may approach the process of creative thinking. Kolb (1981) identified four different types of preferred learning styles:

Divergers: perceive information concretely, process reflectively, are imaginative, believe in their own experience, are insight thinkers, thrive on harmony and personal involvement, seek commitment, meaning, and clarity, and have a high interest in people and culture.
Assimilators: respond to information presented in an organised, logical fashion and benefit if they are given time for reflection. Assimilators perceive abstractly, process reflectively, devise theories, seek continuity, need to know what experts think, love ideas, and are detail oriented.

Convergers: respond to having opportunities to work actively on well-defined tasks and to learn by trial and error in an environment that allows them to fail safely. They perceive abstractly, process actively, integrate theory and practice, are pragmatic, dislike fuzzy ideas, value strategic thinking, are skill oriented, like to experiment, and seek results and applications.

Accommodators: like open-ended questions and to discover things for themselves. They perceive concretely and process actively, learn by trial and error, are interested in self-discovery, are enthusiastic about new things, are adaptable and flexible, like change, are risk-takers, people are important to them.

Divergers and Accommodators are likely to be most at home with generating ideas creative, while Convergers and Assimilators may be happy reflecting on the ideas generated and trying to turn them into more practical suggestions.

Moods, emotions, beliefs, attitudes, experiences, motivations, and experience

Individual moods and emotions can impact on the ability of team members to participate constructively in the creative problem solving process. Both anger and anxiety can have a negative effect on a person's ability to contribute effectively. It is generally considered that being in a happy state of mind is essential. Beliefs, attitudes, experience, motivation, perceptions have a strong impact on a person's ability to be creative and to successfully participate in the creative process.

Perceptions can be strongly influenced by prior beliefs, attitudes, experience, or motivation. A person having such perceptions may be totally unaware of this and the bias it brings with it. Attitudes towards participating in the use of the techniques have to be positive. Motivation to find insights into a problem is essential, and a person's experience will temper whatever ideas arise as a result of any ideation that takes place.

Dealing with an individual's blocks to creativity

Jones (1987) identified four typologies of blocks. These were derived from cluster analysis of self-reported items. The typologies are:

1 *Strategic blocks*: 'one-right-answer approaches,' inflexibility in thinking
2 *Value blocks*: 'over-generalised rigidity influenced by personal values'

3   *Perceptual blocks*: 'over-narrow focus of attention and interest'
4   *Self-image blocks*: poor effectiveness through fear of failure, timidity in expressing ideas, etc.

Jones's approach has resulted in training applications which centre on personal feedback and counselling, including suggestions for the most appropriate mechanisms for developing improved skills.

How techniques help to overcome blocks

Strategic, value, perceptual, and self-image blocks can be overcome to a great extent by use of the techniques themselves. All the techniques lend themselves to facilitating the strategic process of generating ideas. As a result of using the techniques, ideas and insights will be created where none or few existed before. The techniques act as a stimulus to thinking and help evoke, construct, and reconstruct the knowledge and information we hold as individuals in our memory. Where participants engage in group creative problem solving sessions, such as when using brainstorming or synectics, sharing experiences in the group can help build confidence, lessen the risk of making mistakes as individuals, and overcome value prejudices we may hold as individuals. In addition, it can also help compensate for the perceptual blocks and biases we may exhibit as individuals. By sharing a problem with someone else we can appreciate how others might view the same problem and how they might gain insights into the problem. These may well be perspectives that our perceptual bias causes us to overlook.

Working with teams

Usually, this means working with teams led by a facilitator who structures and conducts the ideation. Many managers find it difficult to organise effective creative problem solving teams (McFadzean *et al.*, 1999). Teams may lack direction and focus, they may be uncomfortable with the process, or there may be boredom, discord, or a lack of motivation among the participants. People are most creative when they feel motivated primarily by the interest, enjoyment, satisfaction, and challenge of the work (Amabile, 2013), so it is incumbent on the facilitator to provide such an atmosphere to creative problem solving sessions.

The people who make up the team can help to produce a situation whereby their moods spread through the team (Kelly and Barsade, 2001). Situations can be seen as positive or negative or personally relevant, urgent, or important and suggest something in a situation is good or bad and important or trivial. This could have a negative impact on a creative problem solving exercise.

Group performance may be impeded by the members' fears of being negatively evaluated by the other group members (Camacho and Paulus, 1995). Differences in rank and status among group members can stymie an individual's willingness to contribute for fear of feeling foolish and other personal reasons. A facilitator who is able reduces the group members' concern of being negatively evaluated, and can encourage all group members to believe that their contributions are essential for the group to succeed in its task.

The importance of the facilitator

The success of a creative problem solving session may rest in the hands of the facilitator. McFadzean (2002) argues that desirable facilitator competencies include evoking group creativity, blending all earning and thinking styles: being aware of individual learning/thinking styles; communicating with all styles; drawing out participants of all styles; encouraging creative thinking; accepting all ideas; eliciting the appropriate information from the group participants.

Participation in ideation sessions requires teamwork that exudes confidence and co-operation which will reinforce the team's belief in its capabilities to get to grips with the problem in hand. An effective facilitator would make all group members feel that their efforts are necessary for the group to succeed (Oxley *et al.*, 1996).

Blocks to organisational creative thinking and ways of dealing with them

Management structure has a considerable influence on creativity in an organisation. Top-down management produces centralised decision-making and dissemination of ideas. This can discourage creativity by enforcing disempowered, non-participatory roles on staff who might otherwise make creative contributions (Tsai and Beverton, 2007).

By contrast, bottom-up management leads to employee empowerment as a result of collaboration and shared decision-making (Tsai and Beverton, ibid.). Arguably, there is also greater participation among employees and the creation of an environment for learning, education, and collaboration where people can make use of their creative potential (Cafolla, 2007). Changing to a bottom-up approach to management can be an important step towards removing organisational blocks to creativity.

Some of the major blocks are:

- *Emphasis on managerial control* – control can stifle creativity since autonomy and a degree of freedom are critical ingredients of creative thinking. Moreover, traditional financial controls are not appropriate for long-term innovation efforts
- *Short-range thinking* – there is a tendency to give priority to quick returns with financially measurable results
- *Analysis paralysis* – ideas are often over-analysed, and time is lost along with any competitive advantage
- *Rigid hierarchical structures* – an unpredictable environment requires a responsive organisational structure, and this is not characteristic of most organisations
- *Tendency to look for one project that is likely to generate a big pay-off* – rather than a number of smaller projects with small-to-medium payoffs. Good small projects can thus often be overlooked
- *Market- versus technology-driven product planning* – there tends to be an over-emphasis on market research, in line with the marketing orientation adopted by many companies. While the marketing orientation is very important, it is often implemented at the expense of good ideas which come out of R&D and which never get off the ground
- *Pressure to achieve and do more with fewer resources* – R&D departments are often penalised for cutting costs; the more the department saves one year, the less it has to play with the next. Paradoxically, the more companies have to cut back on expenditure, the more creative they must become
- *Lack of a systematic approach to innovation* – a lack of real ideas about how to innovate
- *Belief that some people are creative* – others are not
- Ways of dealing with such blocks include:
  - Encouraging prudent risk-taking
  - Freedom of thought – some degree of autonomy
  - Linking rewards with specific performance
  - Encouraging different viewpoints on problems
  - Positive involvement of top management
  - Continual flow of ideas
  - Responding positively to new ideas

Elements and conditions of creative organisations

Bessant *et al.* (2001) suggested that everyone in an organisation can in theory make a contribution to problem solving innovation. However, they go on to conclude that most organisations have been operating on beliefs, originating in the 'scientific management' approaches developed at the turn of the century, which see a split into 'thinkers' and 'doers' and which implicitly prevent this from happening.

Questions

1 Why are people sometimes blocked in their thinking? How can they be helped to overcome the various blockages that occur?

2 Why do people find it difficult to solve previously unencountered problems?

3 Tudor Rickards coined the phrase 'mental stuckness.' What exactly did he mean by this phrase, and what is its relevance to the use of creative problem solving methods and techniques?

4 Many organisations and their managers are backward looking. .Assess the impact that this kind of thinking will have on creative thinking and problem solving in an organisation.

5 Picasso said: 'Every act of creation begins with an act of destruction.' How transferable is this notion to the domain of creative problem solving? Discuss.

6 How might making use of each of the following help overcome blocks to creative problem solving?
   - watching a magician at work
   - going to the theatre or the cinema
   - family outings
   - visits to junkyards
   - mixing with or talking to different people – perhaps people whose value systems are different from your own
   - day-dreaming to a sound-effects record
   - free association to music
   - browsing around flea markets
   - scanning old science magazines
   - reading historical accounts
   - reading wants ads
   - indulging in or watching sport
   - studying new subjects through introductory-level books
   - following the news – in the newspapers and on television

7 In what ways is using creative problem solving methods different when working on one's own and when being conducted with teams?

References

Adams, J.L. (1974) *Conceptual Blockbusting*, New York: W. H. Freeman.

Amabile, T.M. (2013) 'Componential theory of creativity', in Kessler, E.H. (ed.), *Encyclopedia of Management Theory*, London, SAGE, 134–139.

Argyle, M. (2001) *The Psychology of Happiness*, New York: Routledge.

Arnold, J.E. (1962) 'Education for innovation', in S.J. Parnes and H.F. Harding (eds), *A Sourcebook for Creative Thinking*, New York: Scribner, 127–138.

Bessant, J., Caffyn, S. and Gallagher, M. (2001) 'An evolutionary model of continuous improvement behaviour', *Technovation*, 21(2), 67–77.

Cafolla, L. (2007) 'Championing change from the bottom up', *China Staff*, 13(7), 2.

Camacho, L.M. and Paulus, P.B. (1995) 'The role of social anxiousness in group brainstorming', *Journal of Personality and Social Psychology*, 68(4), 1071–1080.

Duncker, K. (1945) 'On problem solving (trans. L. S. Lee)', *Psychological Monographs*, 58(5), i–113.

Jones, L.J. (1987) 'The development and testing of a psychological instrument to measure barriers to effective problem solving', unpublished MB.Sc. dissertation, Manchester Business School.

Kelly, J.R. and Barsade, S.G. (2001) 'Mood and emotions in small groups and work teams', *Organizational Behavior and Human Decision Processes*, 86(1), 99–130.

King, L.A., McKee, W.L. and Broyles, S.J. (1996) 'Creativity and the five-factor model', *Journal of Research in Personality*, 30(2), 189–203.

Kirton, M. (1976) 'Adaptors and innovators: a description and measure', *Journal of Applied Psychology*, 61(5), 622–629.

Kolb, D.A. (1981) 'Learning styles and disciplinary differences', in A.W. Chickering (ed.), *The Modern American College*, San Francisco, CA: Jossey-Bass, 85–94.

Luchins, A.A. (1942) 'Mechanisation problem solving: the effect of Einstellung', *Psychological Monographs*, 54 (Whole No. 248).

McFadzean, E.S. (1999) 'Creativity in MS/OR: choosing the appropriate technique', *Interfaces*, 29(5), 110–122.

McFadzean, E.S. (2002) 'Developing and supporting creative problem solving teams: part 2 facilitator competencies', *Management Decision*, 40(6), 537–551.

Oxley, L.N. Dzindolet, M.T. and Paulus, B.Y. (1996) 'The effects of facilitators on the performance of brainstorming groups', *Journal of Social Behavior and Personality*, 11(4), 633–646.

Russ, S.W. (1999) *Affect, Creative Experiences and Psychological Adjustment*, Ann Arbor, MI: Bruner Mazel.

Shapiro, P.J., Weisberg, R.W. and Alloy, L.B. (2000) 'Creativity and bipolarity: affective patterns predict trait creativity', in *Paper Presented at the Convention of the American Psychological Society*, Miami, June.

Tsai, Y. and Beverton, S. (2007) 'Top-down management: an effective tool in higher education?', *International Journal of Educational Management*, 21(1), 6.

Further reading

Bilalić, M., McLeod, P. and Gobet, F. (2008) 'Why good thoughts block better ones: the mechanism of the pernicious Einstellung (set) effect', *Cognition*, 108 (3), 652–661.

Karwowski, M. and Kaufman, J.C. (2017) *The Creative Self: Effect of Beliefs, Self-Efficacy, Mindset, and Identity*, Academic Press.

3 Problem solving

Introduction

The chapter concentrates on problem solving issues before going on to look specifically at creative problem solving itself. The chapter presents a model of problem solving which is put together on the basis of searching the literature on the subject. It then goes on to look at the three types of problems that are encountered and points to how these are tackled in practice. Ill-structured problems in particular are highlighted since it is these types of problems which are best suited to creative problem solving. In addition to being ill-structured, they are often very complex in nature. After reviewing a common-sense approach to problem solving the chapter explains the IDEAL approach put forward by Bransford and Stein. This background to general problem solving is then followed by an introduction to the creative problem solving process.

Nature of problems

Van Gundy (1993) believes 'a problem can be defined as any situation in which a gap is perceived to exist between what is and what should be.' Based on this definition, a problem solving process is one whereby a situation that is not as it should be is changed into one that is as it should be. However, it should be noticed that not all problems require the use of a creative problem solving process (CPS). Indeed, in some cases a CPS process would not be as useful as an existing routine or ready-made solution. These kinds of solutions generally exist for recurring problems, and when it is possible to use one it is often much quicker and more practical.

The testimony of scientists and others indicates that the processes of problem solving are not entirely open to consciousness. One may begin by reasoning consciously and deliberately, but the solution often comes in its own time, suddenly and 'out of nowhere.'

The mathematician Gyorgy Polya introduced the idea that there are general techniques for solving problems, which he called 'heuristics': procedures that often help though they cannot guarantee success. One useful heuristic is working backwards from the solution: if the answer were known, what characteristics would the problem possess? Another important heuristic is to establish sub-goals: think of some situation from which it might be easier to obtain the solution, and work towards that situation first. Still another is means–end analysis: establish lists of methods that are useful for attacking various kinds of goal or sub-goal, and work through the list systematically.

Recent research on problem solving has involved computer programs that enable a computer to solve difficult problems. If the sequence of steps taken by the machine is similar to the sequence reported by human subjects who think aloud, the programme itself can be regarded as a theory of the problem solving process. The programmes developed go through the same sequences of steps (and make the same sorts of errors) as people who are thinking aloud; thus, they probably incorporate many of the principles that govern human problem solving.

It is useful to put together a general model of problem solving as a prior step to looking at the process of creative problem solving. (see Fig 3.1) Problem solving occurs in a multitude of domains and it is perhaps not surprising therefore to note that numerous models appear in the literature to describe the process. In addition, the decision-making literature is also replete with models reflecting interest in the subject in different domains. I have put together the model below to reflect some of the various thoughts and ideas that exist on the matter.

The model indicates that individuals or organisations are constantly scanning their environments. During the scan process they may detect a problem which they feel merits attention. The problem can have any one of three characteristics.

Types of problems

Well-structured – straightforward, familiar to the decision maker, and the
    goal is clear, the information about it is complete
Ill-structured – new/and information about such is ambiguous or incomplete
Programmed – solution is a repetitive decision that can be handled by a
    routine approach (Procedure, rule, policy)

The next step is to properly define the problem before going on to specify and operationalise the goal that needs to be achieved in order to solve the problem. It is anticipated that there may be a number of possible solutions

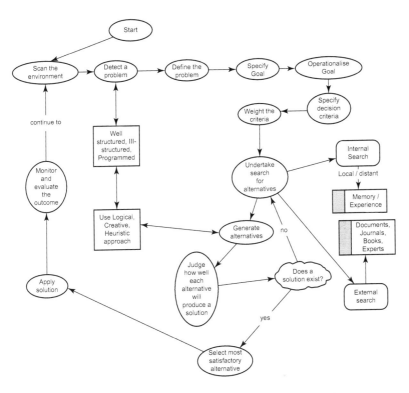

Figure 3.1 A model of the problem solving process

to the problem and one will need to have established decision criteria to enable choice to be made among them. However, it will be first necessary to undertake a search to enable the alternative solutions to be identified. Search may be made on an *internal* or an *external* basis and may be *local* or *distant* in nature. Internal search implies searching people's memories while external search implies looking further afield and consulting papers, books, journals, and even consultants. In the case of internal search there is a tendency to search at a local level or in the area of the problem in the first instance since this will produce solutions quickly if any are to be found. More distant search means looking away from the immediate problem to see if one can locate anything in another domain that may give an insight into the problem.

The search should generate alternatives and may be aided by the creative problem solving techniques in this book in the case of ill-structured problems or by the use of heuristics in the case of programmed problems. In the latter case there are many different kinds of heuristics that may be used (see Kahnemann, 2012). Three major heuristics that are used, however, are discussed below.

Representativeness

The more object X is similar to class Y, the more likely we think X belongs to Y. People predict future performance mainly by similarity of description to future results. For example, when seeking to appoint a new employee, predicting future performance as a manager based on a single reference or interview with the person concerned.

Availability

The frequency of a class or event is often assessed by the ease with which instances of it can be brought to mind. For example, when reviewing the number of expense claims and looking for ways to reduce them, one may more easily recall large claims when these are very much in the minority and have little impact on the overall total of expenses claimed.

Anchoring

People often estimate by adjusting an initial value until a final value is reached. The approach may characterise wage settlements.

The next steps in the process are to judge the most satisfactory solution to the problem, implement it, and monitor how well it serves to provide a solution to the problem. If a satisfactory solution cannot be identified, then a further search has to be undertaken and the latter part of the process repeated.

A common-sense approach to problem solving

Common sense would seem to dictate that a systematic approach is by far the best one to take. One really has to approach a problem with an eye on its context, since the same problem may require a different approach in another situation. One only has to think of how one tackles one's colleagues about different issues to realise that problem solving is contingency based – that is, it varies from situation to situation.

Another important point is that one should never rush to conclusions. Although some problems may seem to require urgent attention, it is better to weigh up alternative causes and outcomes before rushing in headlong in pursuit. has to be made there and then at that moment in times then delay may not be possible. Where one has to time to reflect before having to implement a solution, it is often quite surprising how what is done may differ from the initial diagnosis of the problem.

There are usually a number of steps one has to follow when taking a common-sense approach to solving a problem. ·

The first step is to ensure that one has correctly identified the problem. This may seem unnecessary, yet too often mistakes may be made because the problem has been wrongly diagnosed. In the field of medicine, we some-times hear of wrongly identified breast cancers and subsequent operations which are totally unnecessary. The results of such actions are commonly quite devastating for the patients. So, this is a critical step and needs a great deal of care and attention.

Sometimes one may see multiple problems in a situation. These may vary in terms of importance, from critical to relatively minor and having only low priority as far as the owner of the problem is concerned. It is essential to solve the right problem and one should avoid trying to solve a problem that is seen as low priority or unimportant.

One should seek to identify the problem by asking the right sort of questions or making the best use of one's own powers of observation. Alternatively, there may be special tools, procedures, or even skills that one may need to call upon to ensure that no mistakes are made at this point. In the course of medical diagnosis, for example, GPs conduct initial interviews and examinations of patients and where they consider it necessary, they will refer patients to specialists who can make expert diagnoses of problems. The experts in this instance may make use not only of hi-tech apparatus but also of their specialised experience gained through years of research and previous encounters with similar cases. In a more general sense, it is usually important to explore with the owner of the problem what is leading them to feel there is a problem. One needs to ascertain whether it is something specific, or whether it is an intuitive sense that things aren't as they should be. Getting the owner of the problem to define the problem – with help if necessary – is reassuring for all concerned.

The next step is to analyse the problem. One needs to ascertain how often the problem occurs. Does it happen regularly or only occasionally? Just how inconvenient or severe is the problem? Can one identify the cir-cumstances when the problem arises? Is there anything about these circum-stances which is unusual? Answers to these questions might give one a clue regarding what might be the cause of the problem. Knowing how long it has been going on and whether it has got worse may also assist in making a correct diagnosis of the problem. Problems often affect other processes or people, so exploring this angle can also often be productive in helping to make a correct diagnosis of the problem.

Once these steps have been taken a decision may need to be taken about dealing with the problem. If there seems to be more than one way of dealing with the problem, then it may be necessary to identify the alternatives and then specify decision criteria. Where a number of criteria have to be satisfied it will be important to decide how to weigh the criteria.

It is important to have thought through more than one solution to a problem where this is possible. Terminating the search procedure at the first solution that is identified may be good, but much better solutions may still exist.

When one is confident that one has reached a point where there are diminishing returns to be had from further search, it is necessary to evaluate the options which have been identified. One needs to assess the advantages and disadvantages of each option carefully.

Finding an optimal solution to a problem may be elusive. In many cases it is difficult to determine with any real degree of certainty whether one has found an optimal solution. Often it is a case of selecting the most satisfactory solution. This is referred to as satisficing. Such a solution generally meets all or most of the criteria one has previously set up and scores higher than any of the other alternatives.

Lastly, one has always to allow for contingencies. Despite one's best efforts at selecting a good solution, it may not solve a problem for some reason that one has overlooked. It is therefore important to have several backup solutions as well – just in case!

Various approaches of the problem solving process have been proposed and one of these is shown next.

The problem solving process

Bransford and Stein (1993) proposed a model for improving problem solving skills. The components of the approach are represented by the acronym IDEAL. Where

I = Identify problems and opportunities
D = Define goals
E = Explore possible strategies
A = Anticipate outcomes and act
L = Look back and learn

When trying to solve a problem, the emphasis should be on finding the *first* step rather than on trying to find a complete solution immediately. Having tried out the first step and learned from the experience, one can then proceed to work through subsequent steps. Test marketing is a case in point, where the launch of a new product is done on a gradual basis. Any aspects of the introduction which are less than satisfactory are corrected before the next stage in the roll-out process. Writing and debugging computer programs follows a similar process.

New insights customarily emerge as a product of various pieces of knowledge becoming connected for the first time. It tends to be an evolutionary process where two or more pieces of retained knowledge meld together and then form new insights. This is also true with breakthrough ideas. The knowledge may reside with different people and it is only when they come together and share the knowledge that insights arise. Although an innovation can be based on a new scientific or technical discovery, the recombining of knowledge in the nature of innovations is more common (Hargadon, 2003).

However, finding a way of melding existing knowledge in the hope of discovering a breakthrough may require a very extensive search. Human mental processes use bounded rationality, reflecting limited cognitive ability, so the field of search and the extent of search is limited (Simon, 1996). Since search tends to be local and in the area of the problem, then finding and retrieving material from very distant domains of knowledge is often constrained by established thinking patterns. The majority of people have difficulty in thinking outside of their area of original expertise, because this usually requires them to use a different way of thinking and a different technical language than they are used to.

The context of problem solving

Where the problem solving process appears to fall down, the most frequent cause is not in the problem solving effort itself, but rather in the critical steps that lead up to the problem solving. The critical steps concerned involve

a) Identification of what issues are to be considered as 'problems' to solve
b) Exploring and finally deciding on how to think about the problem
c) Assigning responsibility, naming the team, allocating resources, setting the schedule, and naming key stakeholders
d) The actual effort to solve the problem, understand its cause, design some corrective action, and implement the solution

(Talley, 2013)

Talley (2013) states that after observing hundreds of problem solving efforts in a wide variety of settings he has found the most common 'problem solving discussion' is actually a debate over proposed solutions. One has to be aware of the hazards faced in such a situation. These are aptly summarised in the phenomenon of the *Abiline Paradox and Other Meditations on Management* (Harvey, 1996) where groups in organisations take actions in contradiction to what they really want to do and therefore defeat the very purposes they are trying to achieve. Symptoms of the paradox include the inability to manage agreement and not the inability to manage conflict. This is reflected in organisation members individually agreeing in private about the nature of the situation or problem facing the organisation and what steps would be required to cope with the situation or problem. However, the group members do not accurately communicate their desires and/or beliefs to one another, thereby leading one another into misperceiving the collective reality. Under such circumstances, group members make collective decisions that lead them to take actions contrary to what they want to do.

Problem solving skills

Problem solving skills are important in order to determine the source of a problem and in finding an effective solution.

Some key problem solving skills include:

- Active listening
- Research
- Communication
- Creativity
- Analysis
- Reasoning
- Decision-making
- Dependability

For example:

Active listening

A consultant will need active listening and communication skills when interacting with clients and will also need relevant domain knowledge related to the problem in hand. A consultant will also need to know when to bring in someone with more specialised knowledge relating to a client's problem.

Research

Research skills refer to the ability to gather information about a problem. Some research will need to be undertaken in order to define and solve problems. A search of the World Wide Web may suffice or it may be necessary to conduct field research or an extensive review of the literature relating to the problem. Having research skills is essential when having undertaken problem solving. It will be necessary to identify the cause of the problem and be knowledgeable about the various factors that relate to it. It may also be possible to obtain more information about a problem through discussions with other team members and consulting experts in the field.

Communication

Knowing how to communicate the nature of the problem and possible solutions to others is of paramount importance. It is also essential to know the appropriate communication channels when assistance is required.

Creativity

Many problems require creative insights in order to solve them. If a person has a flair for finding creative solutions then that is a valuable asset. However, skills in creative problem-solving and using its techniques may compensate for any deficiency in natural creativity.

Analysis

Analysis involves examining a problem from all angles. It may include recreating the problem to understand the steps that caused it, and reviewing data that may provide additional details about the problem. Analytical skills help understanding of problems and effectively develop solutions. It will also be necessary to have analytical skills to help distinguish between effective and ineffective solutions.

Reasoning

Reasoning is the ability to use information that has been obtained by research, analysis, and experience to identify steps and draw conclusions. It includes deductive reasoning, which is working backwards from a known conclusion to identify what happened, and inductive reasoning, which is applying evidence that has been obtained to reach conclusions about possible solutions.

Decision-making

It is necessary to reach a decision about how to solve problems that arise. Such decisions may have to be made quickly, so it useful to have a well-rehearsed set of procedures to follow. Having good research and analytical skills can be of enormous help when there is a shortage of experience in those trying to grapple with a problem. One has also to consider that it may be necessary to pass the problem over to someone more capable of solving it.

Dependability

Solving problems in a timely manner is essential. Individuals who can be trusted to both identify and then implement solutions as fast and effectively as possible are highly valued assets.

How to improve problem solving skills

Practice evaluating problems

Evaluate problems from every angle and learn everything you can about each one. Read online help articles, talk to other people who have experienced each one of the problems, and collect as much information as possible.

Isolate the factors

Taking each problem one at a time, isolate different causal factors in that problem to determine what is the source of the problem.

Practice problem solving

Puzzles and practice scenarios are good ways to improve problem solving skills

How to acquire creative problem solving skills

Research has shown continuously over the past 50 years that people can be taught, encouraged and coached or counselled to be more creative. Four basic creative strengths and skills can be easily taught:

1 Fluency – ability to produce many ideas (many of which may be fairly similar or have the same kind of theme)
2 Flexibility – ability to produce a varied mix of ideas (none, or few, of which are similar or share the same kind of underlying theme)
3 Elaboration – ability to add detail, depth, mixtures of viewpoints or perspectives
4 Originality – uniqueness, novelty, newness, creativeness (new), or innovativeness (improvement of existing)
    - Fluency can be developed by holding creative thinking sessions at which ideas for a hundred different uses for everyday objects (sponge, toothpick, eraser, brick, paper-clip, etc.) should be generated. After reaching this number, move on to work-related objects
    - Flexibility can be improved by listing 50 different kinds of uses for everyday objects and then moving on to work on related challenges
    - Elaboration can be developed by describing something (hobby, TV show, tree, cat, athletic event, etc.) in considerable detail, using all the physical senses

- Originality can be learned by picking one common object and listing many new uses for it

Regular practice in each of the above activities can lead to the acquisition of improved creative skills.

Questions

1 Using the common-sense approach to problem solving work, show how you would deal with the following situations:
   - Major fire on the first floor of a five-story office block
   - Discovery of irregularities in expense claims of several of the firm's travelling sales staff
   - Several cases of sexual harassment in the offices by departmental managers
   - Finding new offices for an expanding back office of employees
2 How does the procedure recommended by the Bransford and Stein model differ from the common-sense approach?
3 Repeat the exercise in Question 1 using the nine-stage process for creative problem solving.
   What differences do you notice?
   The formal problem solving process seems to be too simplistic a view of what actually takes place in reality. Can you account for this? Explain.
4 Why should a debate over proposed solutions to a problem be a source of difficulty?
5 Some key problem solving skills are indicated in the text. Can you add any other skills to the list?

References

Bransford, J.D. and Stein, B.S. (1993) *The Ideal Problem Solver*, New York: W. H. Freeman.

Hargadon, A. (2003) *How Breakthroughs Happen: The Surprising Truth about How Companies Innovate*, Boston, MA: Harvard Business School Press.

Harvey, J.B. (1996) *The Abilene Paradox and Other Meditations on Management* (paperback), San Francisco, CA: Jossey-Bass.

Kahnemann, D. (2012) *Thinking Fast and Slow*, London: Penguin.

Simon, H.A. (1996) 'Bounded rationality', in J. Eatwell, M. Milgate and P. Newman (eds), *The New Palgrave Dictionary of Economics*, London: Macmillan.

Talley, J.L. (2013) 'Problem solving process: context of problem solving', available at: http://www.problemsolving2.com/process/theprocess.htm, accessed 26 April 2013.

Van Gundy, A.B. (1993) *Techniques of Structured Problem Solving*, New York: Van Nostrand Reinhold.

Further reading

Robertson, S.I. (2001) *Problem Solving*, East Sussex, UK: Psychology Press.

4 The creative thinking process

Introduction

First, we describe Wallas's model of the creative process, which introduces the idea of the process involved in creative problem solving. We then sketch the formalised model of this process as used as a basis for creative problem solving from ideation through to implementation. The use of ideation techniques is then introduced. We next consider the notion of paradigm shift and how this relates to the choice of a suitable creative problem solving technique that might be used to gain insights into a problem. Finally, we examine analogical thinking and its relevance to problem solving techniques where a substantial paradigm shift is required.

Wallas's model of the creative process

The foregoing looks at the situation as it may occur when we are consciously trying to get insights into a problem. Often, however, we may have a problem which we have still not resolved but which we may in fact be working on at a subconscious level. Graham Wallas (1926) set down a description of what happens as people approach problems with the objective of coming up with creative solutions. He described his four-stage process as follows:

1 In the preparation stage we define the problem, need, or desire, and gather any information the solution or response needs to account for, and set up criteria for verifying the solution's acceptability.
2 In the incubation stage we step back from the problem and let our minds contemplate and work it through. Like preparation, incubation can last minutes, weeks, even years.
3 In the illumination stage, ideas arise from the mind to provide the basis of a creative response. These ideas can be pieces of the whole or the whole itself, that is, seeing the entire concept or entity all at once.

Unlike the other stages, illumination is often very brief, involving a tremendous rush of insights within a few minutes or hours.

4 In verification, the final stage, we carry out activities to demonstrate whether or not what emerged in illumination satisfies the need and the criteria defined in the preparation stage.

It should be noted that research on incubation by Segal (2004) suggests that a break in the attentive activity devoted to a problem may eventually facilitate the solution process. This gives rise to a new hypothesis based on analysis of the structure of insight problems and their solution process. According to this hypothesis, no activity takes place during the break. The break's only function is to divert the solver's attention from the problem, thus releasing her mind from the grip of a false organising assumption. This enables the solver to apply a new organising assumption to the problem's components upon returning to the problem. Moss argues that the process may be influenced by the impact of environmental clues. When a problem is abandoned, a solution may subsequently and unexpectedly emerge. The intervening period, known as incubation, has sometimes been ascribed to opportunity assimilation. According to this theory, impasses to a problem create failure indexes, which ensure that random changes in the environment are detected and utilised.

Cropley's stages model

Cropley (1997) added various stages to Wallas's model. First, he argued that there was a need to recognise or 'find' a problem about which the person can be creative (this is the Preparation Stage). Second, he considered there was a need to communicate the creative outcome to others (this he referred to as the Communication Stage). Third, he envisaged it was necessary to have the outcome judged by people with the relevant cultural background (this he referred to as the Validation Stage). The Preparation Stage makes the process of problem finding more explicit. Creative ideas can be produced without Communication and Validation, but they cannot receive 'socio-cultural validation' (Cropley and Urban, 2000). This may explain why management may sometimes come up with an idea which they think will be good for the workforce only to find that the workforce has a completely different view of it!

   These ideas give rise to the argument that it may be beneficial to structure the process of trying to think creatively at a conscious level in order to generate useful insights into a problem.

The creative problem solving process

Creative problem solving presents a method and techniques for approaching a problem or a challenge in an imaginative and innovative way. It is generally accepted that the creative problem solving process can be broken down into six stages. These six stages are:

Objective finding – define the problem area
Fact finding – gather information
Problem finding – define the problem correctly
Idea finding – generate solutions to the problem.
Solution finding – evaluate and choose between possible solutions
Acceptance findings – implement chosen ideas correctly

(See Parnes, 1992)

Each of these stages involves activities that require, first, divergent thinking, and then convergent thinking. When thinking in a divergent way, the task is to generate as many ideas and solutions as possible. There should be no limits to the ideas that are formed at this stage. Once a satisfactory level of ideas has been reached, convergent thinking must take place. The purpose of this thinking is to focus on obtaining solutions to the problem based on the ideas from the divergent thinking. These activities can be thought of as filling a funnel with ideas that go through a filter. Plenty of ideas are poured in, but only those that are useful and relevant come out. The six-stage process may be extended by the addition of further stages:

constantly analysing the environment
specifying assumptions
controlling to ensure that objectives are achieved post-implementation

The techniques

One of the earliest forms of creative problem solving seems to have been brainstorming (Osborn, 1957). Its origins are somewhat obscure, but in modern times it appears to have been used as a means of focusing attention on finding new insights into problems and decisions at business meetings. A lack of structure and focus in such meetings when it came to making decisions and dealing with problems seemed to suggest that an interesting alternative approach which would evoke participant curiosity and interest might produce beneficial results. During the course of the last half-century or so many different forms of brainstorming have become popular and the idea of a structured approach to creative problem solving has spawned a large variety of techniques (e.g. Morphological Analysis, Lateral Thinking, Synectics, TRIZ, Rich Pictures Vision Building, and many others). Indeed, one has only to review the plethora of techniques that are discussed today in popular management books and on a growing number of internet websites to appreciate the breadth and depth of these techniques.

In some ways it seems to be an anomaly that approaches to structured creative thinking and problem solving should be labelled 'creative.' Creativity is associated with a freedom from thinking in vertical and logical ways so putting a structure onto the process seems to be the very antithesis of what the creative process is all about. Thus, to the sceptical mind it might suggest that one should take a closer look at the techniques that are becoming popular approaches to trying to stimulate the creative process.

Getting stuck in finding a way of dealing with a problem or situation, actual or potential, can lead to unforeseen and undesirable consequences. It is arguably better to put aside time for creative thought than to take some arbitrary or inappropriate action which may subsequently be regretted. Creative problem solving techniques have been suggested by a number of writers in the past and summarised by other in the more recent past. Nevertheless, there are various caveats to bear in mind. While two or more heads may be better than one at generating ideas, experience has shown that getting a group of people to discuss a problem and come up with ideas in an unstructured manner often ends in chaos with no satisfactory outcome. However, the structured approach of creative problem solving techniques provides an answer to this. Indeed, techniques such as brainstorming were thought up to deal with just such a problem and most other techniques are amenable to use by groups of people as well as by individuals on their own. Unfortunately, while brainstorming in particular produces plenty of ideas, these may not necessarily be ones that lead to good insights or good solutions to problems. It has been contended that critical appraisal, debate, and differences of views are more likely to produce good results and that constructive criticism and critical thinking can be even more effective.

There may be some scepticism concerning the usefulness of creative problem solving techniques. Perhaps some teams may have tried to make use of the techniques and found them unhelpful. This chapter addresses why techniques may or may not be helpful. The position with regard to the use of such techniques is complicated because some techniques are more useful for different problems than for others. There is also the point that creative problem solving techniques may not produce a solution to the handling of a situation or a problem. They may just provide new insights into a problem, find new problems, or even nothing at all. Nevertheless, faced with an apparently difficult-to-solve problem, such techniques may offer a way of gaining insights and even finding a solution to the problem.

Paradigm shift and types of creative problem solving techniques

It is argued that in order for useful insights into problems to be obtained attention needs to be given to the degree of paradigm shift that may be required in finding a solution or useful insights (McFadzean, 1998). In many instances preservation of the existing paradigm is possible. However, it may be that a satisfactory insight can only be achieved by stretching or even breaking the paradigm. For example, if we are considering 'how to improve the decor of the offices,' we may be able to do this by making a number of minor modifications to the existing decor as shown in Exhibit 1. This preserves the existing paradigm.

EXHIBIT 1: NO ANALOGIES OR METAPHORS

Checklists

This is the use of questions as spurs to ideation. The simplest checklist comes from the six basic questions:

1 Why is it necessary?
2 Where should it be done?
3 When should it be done?
4 Who should do it?
5 What should be done?
6 How should it be done?

Example

How to improve the decor of the offices
Why? To make dark areas seem lighter
Where? Reception and the main office
When? All year round
Who? For the benefit of office staff and visitors
What? Walls, ceilings
How? Paint the walls and ceilings in bright colours

However, if the problem were to require stretching or even breaking of the paradigm – such as in the case of 'how to vary a food product such as a fishcake and promote it to would-be buyers' then a different kind of approach might be more productive, as indicated in Exhibit 2. In this case a paradigm-stretching approach might provide richer ideas. This might take the form of a personal analogy involving the use of emotions and feelings in order to identify the potential customer with the subject of a problem. The characteristics of the product in this instance are changed and this is within the existing paradigm, but by trying to identify it with satisfying customers' emotions and feelings the paradigm will be stretched. The use of a personal analogy facilitates this process.

EXHIBIT 2: PERSONAL ANALOGY

Personal analogy is the use of emotions and feelings to identify an individual with the subject of a problem. The problem may be how to vary a food product such as a fish-cake and promote it to would-be buyers. It may be boring and may have a fishy odour which may not appeal to people.

Using a personal analogy can involve:

a) describing the object by listing its basic perceived characteristics which relate to the problem – e.g. appear boring, fishy odour, does not appeal to people

b) describing the emotions, the object might have in a given situation – e.g. dull, sad, dejected, stodgy

c) describing how someone feels when using the object – disappointed, uncomfortable, cheap

d) describing what it feels like to be the given object – stodgy, cheap, tasteless

This may lead to some new element such as a cheese- or tomato-sauce filling being added to the product to counter the undesirable characteristics and a promotional image and message featuring desirable emotions and feelings to be associated with the new product.

Where preservation of a paradigm is concerned, classical brainstorming, morphological analysis and listing, and many techniques not requiring analogical reasoning might be deemed suitable. This included such things as improving products or services by listing their features or dimensions and considering other ways in which these might be provided (Exhibit 1). This kind of technique is simple to use and should not pose any difficulty for anyone using it.

However, where greater degrees of paradigm shift are required they may demand the use of techniques needing some degree of analogical reasoning. These techniques might include Synectics (Gordon, 1961; Nolan, 2003) and the use of metaphors. Using these approaches often involves identifying features and dimensions of an analogous problem for which solutions are known and then relating these known solutions back to the given problem in order to gain appropriate insights (Exhibit 2). This is more challenging and more time-consuming. Finding an appropriate analogy or metaphor requires a degree of thought. In addition, the use of analogy can range from the simple case illustrated in Exhibit 2 to much more sophisticated and even abstract analogies. In the case of Synectics, one may have to progress through several analogies before reaching any potentially useful ideas. Techniques involving the use of analogies or metaphors are best used in a group problem solving exercise with a person experienced in leading a group in order to get the maximum benefit from using the technique.

The aim of these techniques is to help a team think creatively when they find themselves stuck on a problem and unable to find an effective way of dealing with it. However, it is important to understand the purpose and limitations of such techniques. Essentially, creative problem solving techniques simply give new perspectives on a problem. Such a new perspective may lead to a course of action or a solution to a problem or it may simply lead to a different way of perceiving or defining a problem. It is of paramount importance that these limitations are understood. However, it is likely that their use can help generate new perspectives and insights into a situation or problem. A useful paper by Vernon, Hocking, and Tyler (2016) reviewed the literature and gives practical evidence of the use of most the techniques and their usefulness.

Analogical reasoning

Blevins and Blevins (2009) argue that people are constantly looking for patterns in what they observe and once these are identified they are then related to other patterns that people have observed and are employed to predict further patterns and similarities. The analogical reasoning that underpins them demands the recognising of structural similarities between what are perceived to be dissimilar elements. Similarities may be highly abstract, involving functional and causal relationships.

Gentner and Colhoun (2010) posit that there are five steps one has to follow when undertaking analogical thinking:

1 Retrieval: accessing a prior similar or analogous example for comparison with the problem in hand from long-term memory
2 Mapping: aligning the representational structures to derive the commonalities and projecting inferences from one analog to the other
3 Evaluation of the analogy and its inferences
4 Abstraction of the structure common to both analogies

5 Re-representation: adaptation or of one or both representations to improve the match

Retrieval is the most challenging step in the process. There is considerable evidence that similarity-based retrieval, unlike the mapping process, is more influenced by surface similarity than structural similarity. Strong surface similarity and content effects seem to dominate what is recalled. Thus, too often, analogies may be extracted from long-term memory which are inappropriate for the problem in hand while others in long-term memory are overlooked. It is suggested that one remedy for poor relational retrieval is to make greater use of analogy during learning and reasoning.

Looking at the creative problem solving techniques illustrated in this book one will recognise that many of them directly employ analogical thinking in one way or another. One will appreciate from the foregoing that appropriate choice of analogy for a problem is critical to whether the technique is likely to produce any useful insights into a problem.

The process requires the identification of both surface similarities and structural similarities between the focal problem and the analogue problem. Surface similarity describes the resemblance of the focal problem to the analogue problem while structural similarity may be found if relations between elements of the analogue problem are similar to relations between various elements of the focal problem.

Structural similarity is essential if the analogy is to have any value in helping to solve a focal problem (Blanchette and Dunbar, 2000).

In the next chapter we will emphasise the importance of the creative problem solving process as a useful aid by examining reasons why people have difficulty in coming up with creative ideas.

Questions

1 It might be suggested that Wallas's model of the creative process can be related to the steps in the creative problem solving process. To what extent would you agree or disagree with this?
2 A six- and nine-step model is proposed for the creative problem solving process. When would the nine-step process be most appropriate?
3 How is paradigm shift related to the kind of problem solving techniques that might best be employed on a problem?
4 Indicate the main difficulties that might be encountered when using analogies. How can you be sure that you have found a suitable analogy to use with a problem?
5 Evaluate the suitability of the analogy used in the problem in Exhibit 2. Can you think of another analogy?

References

Blanchette, I. and Dunbar, K. (2000) 'How analogies are generated: the roles of structural and superficial similarity', *Memory & Cognition*, 28(1), 108–124.

Blevins, J.P. (2009) 'Introduction: analogy in grammar', in J. P. and J. Blevins (eds), *Analogy in Grammar: Form and Acquisition*, Oxford: Oxford University Press.

Cropley, A.J. (1997) 'Fostering creativity in the classroom', in M.A. Runco (ed.), *The Creativity Research Handbook*, Vol. 1, Cresskill, NJ: Hampton Press, pp 83–114.

Gentner, D. and Colhoun, J. (2010) 'Analogical processes in human thinking and learning', in B. Glatzeder, V. Goel and A. von Müller (eds), *On Thinking, vol. 2: Towards a Theory of Thinking*, Berlin: Springer-Verlag, 35–48.

Gordon, W.J. (1961) *Synectics*, New York: Harper & Row.

McFadzean, E.S. (1998) 'Enhancing creative thinking within organisations', *Management Decision*, 36(5), 309–315.

Nolan, V. (2003) 'Whatever happened to synectics', *Creativity and Innovation Management*, 12(1), 24–27.

Osborn, A. (1957) *Applied Imagination: Principles and Procedures of Creative Thinking*, New York: Scribner.

Parnes, S. J. (1992) *Source Book for Creative Problem-solving*, Buffalo, NY: Creative Foundation Press.

Segal, E. (2004) 'Incubation in insight problem-solving incubation', *Creativity Research Journal*, 16(1), 141–148.

Vernon, D., Hocking, I. and Tyler, T.C. (2016) 'An evidence-based review of creative problem-solving tools a practitioner's resource', *Human Resource Development Review*, 15(2), 230–259.

Wallas, G. (1926) *The Art of Thought*, London: Jonathan Cape.

Further reading

Jalil, P.A. (2007) 'Working memory, cerebellum, and creativity, institute of academic development and training', *Creativity Research Journal*, 19(1), 39.

Mumford, M.D., Medeiros, K.E. and Partlow, P.J. (2012) 'Creative thinking: processes, strategies, and knowledge', *Journal of Creative Behavior*, 46(1), 30–47.

Raichie, M. (2010) 'The brain's dark energy', *Scientific American*, 302(3), 44–49.

5 Objective finding, fact finding, and problem finding – definitions

Introduction

Establishing and defining the problem is probably the most important stage of the creative problem solving process, for unless the problem is correctly defined it is unlikely that a truly satisfactory solution to it can be found. The objective finding stage essentially involves 'divergent thinking to generate a list of problems one is facing.' Convergence is then used to identify the most relevant problem areas for further exploration. 'Hits' and 'hotspots' are identified by questioning 'ownership' (is one motivated to solve it?); priority (how important is the problem?); and critical nature (how urgent is it to solve this problem?). Next is the fact finding stage, where overall comprehension of the problem is increased by collection of relevant information. This also helps new ideas to be generated. 'Hits' and 'hotspots' can assist convergence here. The previously identified problem(s) may now be seen from a new perspective. There are a variety of problem definition mechanisms. They can be considered as either redefinition approaches or analytical approaches. First, we look at redefinition approaches. The techniques we consider here include laddering, goal orientation, boundary examination, progressive abstractions, and the 'why' method. Under the heading of analytical methods, we look at decomposable matrices and cause-and-effect diagrams.

Stressing the importance of objective finding, fact finding, and gaining different perspectives on a problem can itself sometimes alleviate blocked thinking. The problem we start off with is not necessarily the one which we should try to solve. It is quite possible that if we try to solve the problem as we initially perceive it then either it won't be solved to our satisfaction or the solution we implement will only provide temporary relief to the problem. Quite often we are apt to treat symptoms rather than getting to grips with the real problem itself.

Objective finding

Constant environmental analysis and problem recognition

Executives and managers have to be constantly on the lookout for problems and might be able to identify them in one of a number of ways:

1 By comparing current experiences with past experiences
2 By comparing current experiences with current objectives or plans
3 By comparing performance with models of desirable outcomes
4 By comparing performance with that of other organisations or subunits
(Pounds, 1969)

Pounds noted that the most commonly used approach was the first and that the third and fourth were rarely used. Some business problems require extensive study because they seem likely to uncover the possibility of producing profitable marketing opportunities or, conversely, sizeable losses. Some will require immediate attention while others may be less urgent.

Kipling's Checklist

The six honest serving men method (Parnes *et al.*, 1981) is perhaps most useful in the fact finding stage, although it can be applied usefully at other stages. The technique involves asking such questions as:

Who will be ...?
What will they ...?
Where will they ...?
When should it be ...?
How will they ...?
Why will they ...?

The steps are as follows:

1 State the problem in the format ... In what ways might ...? (IWWM ...?).
2 Write down separate list of Who? What? Where? When? Why? and How? questions relevant to the problem.
3 Examine responses to each question and use as a stimulus to generate problem redefinitions.
4 Record problem redefinitions generated in (3) above.
5 Select the best redefinition for ideation purposes.

Much of this kind of information can be obtained from scanning documents and reports and attending meetings. In addition many of those involved in problem solving will have this information in their heads. It is necessary to get the information out into the open.

Example

The problem concerns low staff morale in a supermarket chain.

1   IWWM we improve staff morale?
2   Who are the people concerned?

Shop service counter staff

What is low morale?
Lack of motivation to do a good job and present a friendly interface with the customer
Where does the problem seem to persist?
In all city-centre locations
When is the problem most in evidence?
At weekends
Why should one try to raise morale?
To improve the customer-service interface and encourage more customers to shop at weekends
How can morale be heightened?
By finding out how best to satisfy the wants and needs of staff

The foregoing might produce the following problem redefinitions:

IWWM we satisfy the wants and needs of weekend retail counter staff in city-centre stores?
IWWM we seek to improve the friendliness of the customer service interface?

Problem finding – definition

The problem finding stage encourages one to consider a variety of problem perspectives. Restating the problem might unlock a new viewpoint that can lead to many creative solutions. To create these viewpoints, the group examines the information obtained during fact finding to generate possible problem redefinitions. A systematic approach to problem definition can help and direct staff in their efforts to obtain relevant information. In addition, it is also informative to all those people in the organisation who will be affected by the findings and recommendations.

Problem definition must take into account the situation of the company and its ability to take sound action. Poorly thought-out decisions can cause major problems, sometimes with disastrous consequences. Many things can go wrong, and many opportunities can be missed. The executives in the firm need to anticipate and prevent as many of these as possible, and in each case the first action should be a precise definition of the problem.

Problems arise all the time in business. Some are vitally important problems and concern sales, profits, and the general welfare of the business. A well-planned statement of the problem has to be thought through. Since different executives may have different perspectives on the problem, and hence different views as to its precise nature, there is a need to consult everyone concerned before the problem is finally fully specified. Each individual must contribute his or her thoughts to the problem definition before a valid, useful study of the problem can be properly undertaken.

Redefinition approaches

There are a number of methods which come under this heading. The main idea behind these approaches is to enable the problem solver to gain new perspectives on the problem.

Getting perspectives on a problem

Two useful approaches to problem definition are suggested by Rickards. The first involves the practising of getting different perspectives, while the second, a technique called 'laddering,' provides a useful method for gaining perspectives on actual problems.

Practising perspective getting

Generate a wide variety of scenarios which are readily 'visible in the mind's eye.' Try to make the scenarios ambiguous in nature. Describe the scenario in three or four sentences and then get people to suggest some possible problem perspectives.

Example

Sam is early for work.
He is searching his desk.
The desk is very untidy.
He repeatedly examines the drawers.

Possible problem perspectives:

How to find whatever is missing.
How to tidy the desk.
How to arrange things in the office so nothing gets mislaid.
An alternative approach, suggested by the author, is to use pictures where the situation is ambiguous and ask people to identify problem perspectives.

Laddering

Perspectives can come in varying degrees of complexity. One can think of them as occupying different heights on a ladder. It is often useful to consider where you are on a ladder and whether it would be worthwhile going up to higher levels of generality or down to levels of specifics. The ladder can have many rungs, but we can think of the ladder as having a top portion, a middle portion, and a bottom portion. At the top we find the strategic or conceptual level, in the middle we find the operational and managerial level, while at the bottom we find the immediate and fix-it-quick level.

For any situation with which one is familiar it should be possible to find all three levels on the ladder. Asking the question Why? moves one up the ladder while asking the question How? helps one to move down the ladder.

Example

Consider some perspectives faced by a sales manager trying to expand sales:

How to improve sales techniques (high level) How to provide sales training (middle level) How to produce a sales manual (low level).
Laddering is useful for exploring and resetting perceived boundaries of a problem investigation. It helps to avoid too narrow a band of perspectives.

Goal orientation

Goal orientation is a redefinitional technique which assists us in obtaining a correctly defined problem. It has five stages, the first of which is to work out a general outline of the problem. Suppose that the problem with which we are confronted relates to falling sales experienced after the entrance of a new competitor into the market. In this case we might accept this as the general statement of the problem. The second step is to work out what the goal is: where the organisation wants to be after solving the problem. This might be to regain the previous level of sales. The next steps are to work out what obstacles and constraints the organisation must face in order to reach the goal. An obstacle might be that only limited funding is available from within the firm to put an idea into practice. A constraint might be that the existing prices of products need to be maintained since cuts or rises in prices are not considered to be practical considerations for competitive reasons. The final stage is to come up with a new problem statement. This might be:

'How to get more people to buy our products without reducing or raising prices or being reliant on funds from within the firm.'

Once the problem is correctly defined, we can move on to the next stage of the process – idea finding.

Boundary examination

Boundary examination (de Bono, 1971) encourages one to take a fresh look at the assumptions one is making with respect to a problem. Through re-examining the assumptions one can gain a new perspective on a problem. The process is as follows:

1 One writes down an initial statement of the problem.
2 Important words and phrases in the statement are highlighted and examined for any hidden assumptions.
3 Important connotations of assumptions are identified, without considering the relevance of assumptions.
4 Any new problem definition that is implied is recorded.

Example

A firm wants to reduce costs of producing and marketing its goods so as to be more competitive in the marketplace.

1   In what ways might the company reduce costs of producing and marketing its goods so as to be more competitive in the marketplace?
2   In what ways might the company reduce costs of producing and marketing its goods so as to be more competitive in the marketplace?
3   a) company reduces costs – assumes that the firm can reduce costs and it is necessary to do so
b) production and marketing – assumes that the focus of the problem is here

    c) more competitive in the marketplace – assumes the firm is not competitive enough

4   a) company reduces costs and

    b) production and marketing were taken as the key assumptions. It was felt that the real problem lay not in reducing costs or in more efficient production and marketing but in making the product more attractive to customers. This led to the redefinition: How to make the product more attractive to customers?

Boundary examination can produce thought-provoking problem definitions. However, there are no clear guidelines for indicating how boundary assumptions should be examined.

Progressive abstractions

The method was suggested by Geschka *et al.* (1973) and allows one to make different problem definitions by employing progressively higher levels of problem abstraction until a satisfactory definition of the problem is attained. It is similar to the laddering technique mentioned earlier in the chapter. In essence it relies on repeatedly trying to identify the essential problem through a series of abstractions from problem redefinitions. The steps are:

1 Write down a general statement of the problem.
2 Generate possible problem solutions by asking the question: What is the essential problem?
3 New problem definitions are developed from the answers produced at (2).
4 (2) and (3) are repeated until the solutions begin to exceed existing skills and technological resources and/or until the solutions are outside one's sphere of influence.
5 Select a satisfactory problem definition for the purpose of generating ideas.

Example

1   How to improve meetings?
2   IWWM we improve meetings?
    a)   have at the most convenient times
    b)   circulate agendas well in advance
    c)   have better-structured meetings

3   IWWM we schedule meetings at the most convenient times for people?
   a) use diary facilities on email to find times when people have other recorded commitments
   b) invite only people for whom the meetings are highly relevant
4   IWWM we invite only people for whom the meetings are highly relevant?
   a) keep a detailed list of people's interests and update regularly on the network

The abstractions are continued until either a working solution or a number of solutions can be found or until answers seem to be impractical. In the above example it will be noted that only a part of the possible progressive abstractions has been illustrated. At Stage (3), for example, one could ask 'IWWM we have better-structured meetings,' and of course there are also other possible progressive abstractions at Stage (1) than the one selected for illustration.

'Why' method

This method really reflects the 'why' dimension of the laddering technique mentioned earlier in the chapter. The method again relies on changing the level of abstraction and was suggested by Parnes (1981). As we noted earlier, changing the level of abstraction leads to new perspectives. The method is useful for broadening a problem and exploring its various boundaries. It also helps the user to appraise basic goals and objectives. The following steps should be followed:

State the problem.
Ask why it is that one wants to do whatever is stated in the problem.
Answer the question posed in Step (2).
Use the answer to redefine a new problem question.
Repeat Stages (2) and (3) until a high level of problem abstraction is achieved.

Example

IWWM we improve the performance of car tyres?
Question: Why do we want to improve the performance of car tyres?
Answer: To improve tyre road-handling under adverse conditions
Redefinition: IWWM we improve tyre road-handling under adverse conditions?

Question: Why do we want to improve tyre road-handling under adverse conditions?

Answer: To make cars safer to drive

Redefinition: IWWM we make cars safer to drive?

Question: Why do we want to make cars safer to drive?

At this point we have gone too far with the level of abstraction. We could redefine the problem as: How can we improve the performance of car tyres to make cars safer to drive?

Analytical techniques

Decomposable matrices

If it is possible to view the subject of a problem as a complex hierarchical system, then this form of analysis can be employed (Simon, 1969). It involves breaking down the system under study into its various sub-systems. The method employed is as follows:

1 Establish that the subject of the problem can be viewed as a hierarchical set of sub-systems – organisations, groups of people, the human body, many different products, production processes, marketing strategies, etc., can be viewed as such systems.
2 List the major sub-systems and their components.
3 Enter the sub-systems and their components into a diagonal matrix such that it is possible to identify cells representing the interaction of one sub-system with another.
4 Use a five-point scale to represent the importance of the interaction or strength of the relationship between and within the sub-systems.
5 Select the highest-weighted interactions for further analysis or generation of ideas.

Example

Problem: How to improve the customer service level of an organisation.

1   An organisation is suitable for this form of analysis – it is a complex hierarchical system comprising a number of sub-systems.
2   The major sub-systems and their attributes/features are:

The customer service level:

a)   effectiveness
b)   friendliness
c)   reliability
d)   speed

e)   complaint handling
f)   efficiency
g)   capacity

Infrastructure sub-system:

a)   decision-making structures
b)   administrative structures
c)   policies, operating procedures, and protocols.
d)   human resources, recruitment, and staff selection
e)   training system
f)   supervisory and coaching system
g)   information system and data supports

Communication sub-system:

a)   external
b)   internal

2 Matrix

Here, for reasons of space, we shall consider interactions between the three
sub-systems: customer service, infrastructure, and communication
     Notes

CS = Customer service
I = Infrastructure
C = Communication

Scores of 5 within the same sub-system are shown in bold (**5**). Where high
scores at the interface between sub-systems occur these will be seen as
of great interest and key areas for further exploration. For example, most
aspects of infrastructure and communication are picked out as very important in relation to customer service.

Cause-and-effect diagrams

The problem first identified here is the high absenteeism rate. We look for
causes, effects, and associations and produce a map or diagram (Figure 5.2).
The next stage involves picking out those causes and effects which seem to
be central to the problem under study. If something is too far removed from
the central problem, it is discarded. In Figure 5.2, the boxes relating to orders
and repeat sales are peripheral to the central problem and so are discarded.
The remaining boxes, however, may be taken either as suitable redefinitions
of the original problem or as starting-points for further exploration.

| | C S | | | | | | | I | | | | | | | C | |
	A	B	C	D	E	F	G	A	B	C	D	E	F	G	A	B
A	-	3	2	5	3	1	4	5	4	5	4	1	2	1	4	4
B	-	-	2	2	4	2	4	3	3	1	1	2	1	2	1	1
Customer **C**	-	-	-	1	1	1	1	5	5	2	5	5	5	5	4	5
Service **D**	-	-	-	-	1	1	4	5	5	5	5	2	1	3	3	2
E	-	-	-	-	-	1	4	3	5	2	2	2	4	3	1	1
F	-	-	-	-	-	-	1	5	5	5	4	4	5	5	5	5
G	-	-	-	-	-	-	-	5	3	2	2	2	4	3	1	1
A	-	-	-	-	-	-	-	-	5	5	5	3	4	3	5	5
B	-	-	-	-	-	-	-	-	-	1	5	2	2	5	5	3
Infrastructuure **C**	-	-	-	-	-	-	-	-	-	-	1	1	1	1	1	1
D	-	-	-	-	-	-	-	-	-	-	-	1	1	5	5	5
E	-	-	-	-	-	-	-	-	-	-	-	-	1	1	1	1
F	-	-	-	-	-	-	-	-	-	-	-	-	-	1	1	1
G	-	-	-	-	-	-	-	-	-	-	-	-	-	-	1	1
Communication **A**	-	-	-	-	-	-	-	-	-	-	-	-	-	-	-	5
B	-	-	-	-	-	-	-	-	-	-	-	-	-	-	-	-

Figure 5.1 A decomposable matrix

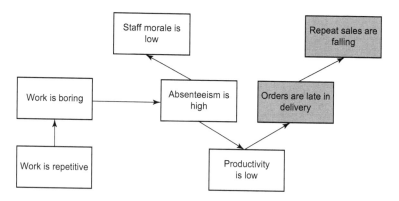

Figure 5.2 Cause-and-effect diagram

A note of caution

While people should be encouraged to understand a problem before generating ideas, if they do this too thoroughly, they run the risk corrupting any potential ideas they may generate. Problem definition is a catch-22 situation ending in a paradox.

Greater analysis of a problem leads to greater understanding of it. This may produce fresh perspectives but it may inhibit getting unique ideas. Knowing too much can lead to conventional solution proposals.

To overcome this problem Gordon (1961) suggested describing a general, abstract problem without revealing the 'real' problem. This abstract problem should have the general principle underlying the real problem. The participants should then be asked to generate ideas for the abstract problem. The process should then be followed by repeating it for a slightly less abstract, more specific version of the real problem. This process may be repeated again with an even more specific version of the real problem. Finally, the real problem should be revealed and the ideas for the two abstract problems used as stimuli for new ideas.

It is suggested here that since the process is a fairly long one it might be reserved for situations where over-analysis and familiarity with the problem are an issue. Moreover, it is an approach which users may find more suitable to use with some creative problem solving techniques than others, e.g. brainstorming.

Questions

1 'The solution to a problem lies in its definition. 'To what extent would you agree or disagree with this statement? Why?

2 How can one try to make sure that one has correctly defined a problem?

3 Why is it often desirable to undertake problem redefinition when trying to find solutions for a problem? Take any management problem which you consider has many possible solutions and outline two methods which might be used to help redefine the problem.

4 A civil engineering project involves constructing a road through a crocodile-infested swamp. Experience to date shows that the crocodiles present a considerable hazard to human life and threaten the completion of the project within the time schedule. Failure to complete within the scheduled time period will incur penalties of the order of £1,000,000 per day. Suggest different perspectives on the problem using the laddering technique.

5 In order to define a problem it is first necessary to recognise that a problem exists, to identify objectives, and establish facts relating to the

problem. Illustrate how you would do this with regard to a problem of your choice.

6   Show how dimensional analysis might be used to define the limits, boundaries, and dimensions of a problem relating to inroads being made into your markets by competition.

7   Using a management problem of your choice show how you might use the following methods to help with defining the problem:
   a)   goal orientation
   b)   boundary examination
   c)   progressive abstractions

8   Illustrate with a suitable example how you might use decomposable matrices.

9   Consider how you might use cause-and-effect diagrams in dealing with previously unencountered problems. What are the main difficulties you might expect to encounter?

References

de Bono, E. (1971) *Lateral Thinking for Management*, New York: McGraw-Hill (republished in Pelican).

Geschka, H., Schaude, G.R. and Schlicksupp, H. (1973) 'Modern techniques for solving problems', *Chemical Engineering*, 80(18), 91–97.

Gordon, W.J. (1961) *Synectics*, New York: Harper & Row.

Parnes, S.J. (1981) *The Magic of Your Mind*, Buffalo, NY: Creative Education Foundation/Bearly.

Pounds, W.F. (1969) 'The process of problem solving', *Industrial Management Review (Fall)*, 11, 1–19.

Simon, H.A. (1969) *The Science of the Artificial*, Cambridge, MA: MIT Press.

Further reading

Chand, I. and Runco, M.A. (1993) 'Problem finding skills as components in the creative process', *Personality and Individual Differences*, 14(1), 155–162.

Hocking, I. and Vernon, D. (2017) 'The right tool for the right task: structured techniques prove less effective on an ill-defined problem finding task', *Thinking Skills and Creativity*, 26, 84–91.

Lee, H. and Cho, Y. (2007) 'Factors affecting problem finding depending on degree of structure of problem presentation', *Journal of Education & Research*, 101, 113–124.

Reiter-Palmon, R. and Robinson, E.J. (2009) 'Problem identification and construction: what do we know, what is the future?', *Psychology of Aesthetics, Creativity and the Arts*, 3(1), 43–47.

6   Idea generating
– non-analogical

Introduction

In this chapter the techniques we look at are essentially systematic structuring mechanisms designed to facilitate the gaining of insights into the problem. A variety of techniques are considered, including checklists, listing, morphological analysis, brainstorming, and aspects of lateral thinking. If the subject of a problem has one or more easily identifiable dimensions, most of these techniques may be useful tools for helping to generate ideas. The techniques examined here are essentially paradigm-preserving techniques and do not require the use of analogical thinking. Most people should find these techniques extremely easy to use. While the techniques are essentially structuring mechanisms, and at first sight appear to be at variance with the nature of creativity, they do afford the facility to undertake unassisted ideation within the structures that they offer.

Checklists

This is the use of questions as spurs to ideation. The simplest checklist comes from the six basic questions:

1 Why is it necessary?
2 Where should it be done?
3 When should it be done?
4 Who should do it?
5 What should be done?
6 How should it be done?

Example

How to create a friendly atmosphere at work:

Why?: to make it easier to communicate with colleagues and get work done.
Where?: especially in meetings where staff of all grades are present.
When?: prior to the meetings taking place.
Who?: the departmental manager.
What?: tell all staff how a meeting should be conducted and what is expected of them.
How?: a booklet or leaflet circulated to all staff for guidance.

Another suggestion involves asking the following questions:

Adapt? Minimise/eliminate?
Modify? Rearrange?
Substitute? Reverse?
Magnify/maximise? Combine?
(See SCAMPER proposed by Alex Faickney Osborn (1957) and further developed by Bob Eberle (1996))

In addition, the following might also be applied:

Add/subtract something.
Vary shape.
Change colour.
Change size.
Vary materials.
Modify design or style.
Rearrange parts.

The technique facilitates idea generation by having one prepare a list of items related to a problem and checking the items against certain aspects of the problem. It can be used both as a problem-delineation list and as a solution-finding list. The purpose of the former is to provide a direction for the idea search, to make sure that no ideas have been overlooked, and to evaluate the applicability of ideas borrowed from a previous problem. Checklists used for possible solutions are concerned with developing new ideas. The most common use of checklists involves identifying new product ideas by making alterations to existing products.

Problem-solution checklists are a simple method of preventing the oversight of obvious solutions to a problem. They also enable previous solutions to be adapted to current problems. In order to be effective, the technique is best used as a supplement to more open-ended techniques.

Attribute listing

Attribute listing is a good technique for ensuring that all possible aspects of a problem have been examined. Attribute listing involves breaking the problem down into smaller and smaller bits and seeing what can be discovered as a result.

Example

Let's say you are in the business of making torches. You are under pressure from your competition and need to improve the quality of your product. By breaking the torch down into its component parts – casing, switch, battery, bulb, and the weight (the attributes of each one) – you can develop a list of ideas and you can improve each one (Table 6.1).

Attribute listing is a very useful technique for quality improvement of complicated products and procedures for services. It is a good technique to use in conjunction with some other creative techniques, especially idea-generating ones like brainstorming. This allows you to focus on one specific part of a product or process before generating a whole lot of ideas.

Morphological analysis

Morphological analysis (Zwicky,1948; Allen, 1962) is a tool which can help generate a vast number of ideas. It works best as a visual aid. However, this can prove difficult in circumstances where the problem is complex. Ideally, the problem should have two or three dimensions to permit the construction of two-dimensional or three-dimensional grids.

First, possible dimensions are listed which describe the problem or system being studied. No more than three dimensions can be represented diagrammatically, and they must be relevant and have a logical interrelationship. For example, if an organisation decides to alter its product in response to changing requirements, it may consider product shape and the material out of which the product can be made as two such dimensions. In this case the dimensions would be represented on a two-dimensional

Table 6.1 Attribute listing: Improving a torch

Feature	Attribute	Ideas
Casing	Plastic	Metal
Switch	on/off	on/off/low beam
Battery	Consumable	Rechargeable
Bulb	Glass	Plastic
Weight	Heavy	Light

grid (or on a cube for three dimensions), and a list of attributes is then generated under each dimension. Free-wheeling and offbeat ideas are encouraged.

The next step is to examine combinations of attributes across the dimensions, however unusual or impractical they may seem. For example, a cross may be put in a box if the combination is used at present and a nought if it is a potential one worth pursuing. Promising ideas are then subsequently evaluated for their suitability.

When considering more than three, a variation called 'morphological forced connections' may be applied. This uses a two-dimensional grid with the dimensions written across the top columns, and the attributes, or ways that they can be accomplished, written in the cells beneath. A combination is represented by a line linking a cell from each column.

Example

Suppose a firm wants to generate ideas for a new educational toy for toddlers. The first stage is to identify suitable categories of ideas to use as axes of a matrix, bearing in mind that one is seeking to discover opportunities rather than come up with an immediate solution. The chosen dimensions must be relevant to the problem and have some logical interrelationship. However, the items listed under each dimension can be as offbeat as one wants. The morphology identifies the dimensions which describe the toy and then identifies lists of attributes under each dimension (see Table 6.2 for example).

In the example given in Table 6.2, the attributes of each dimension can be combined with each other, thus giving 9x8x9 = (648) possibilities. Sometimes it may be necessary to consider three or even four dimensions, but this makes the task of evaluating ideas laborious, and so the two or three most important dimensions are usually chosen.

Table 6.2 Morphological analysis: A new toy for a child

Material	Where used	Educational purpose
Felt	Cot	Alphabet
Rubber	Pram	Numbers
Plastic	Playpen	Shapes
Wood	Beach	Sounds
Transparent Perspex	Car	Colours
Wool	Bath	Textures
Metal	Garden	Co-ordination
Inflatable plastic	Holidays	Smell
Luminescent		Construction

Brainstorming and its variants

Brainstorming is perhaps the most popular of the creative problem solving techniques. It essentially encourages people to work within existing paradigms though the introduction of wild ideas may, on occasion, lead to paradigm stretching by moving the thought processes of participants away from the problem in hand. It is a technique which should appeal to most participants irrespective of whether they are essentially divergent or convergent thinkers.

In a group situation having a mixed range of thinking styles, learning styles and personalities can be advantageous, and in addition, one should bear in mind the caveat regarding group dynamics.

Classical brainstorming

Osborn (1957) advocated the virtue of 'deferment of judgment' as an aid to creativity. Later work at Buffalo in the United States by Parnes (1963) supported Osborn's claims that, through the deferment-of-judgement principle, more and more good ideas could be produced in unit time. Osborn had four basic rules for brainstorming:

1 Criticism is not permitted – adverse judgement of ideas must be withheld.
2 Free-wheeling is welcome – the wilder the idea the better. One should not be afraid to say anything that comes into one's mind.

This complete freedom stimulates more and better ideas.

3 Quantity is required – the greater the number of ideas, the more likelihood of winners.
4 Combinations and improvements should be tried out. In addition to contributing ideas of one's own, one should suggest how ideas of others can be improved, or how two or more ideas can be joined into a still better idea.

Brainstorming can be used to help find solutions to many different kinds of open-ended problem: for example, trouble-shooting problems (how to reduce downtime on the production line; how to reduce shoplifting in the store) and problems where a large number of ideas are required (identifying new product concepts; new market/segment concepts; names for products or companies). Unsuitable problems might include those which require technical or professional expertise beyond the capability of the members of the group or those which have only one answer.

Rules of brainstorming

Brainstorming is a tool to generate ideas, and some ground rules are needed to maintain order. The following four rules will maximise productivity:

Evaluate later.
Encourage wild ideas.
Go for quantity.
Build on other ideas.

The process of brainstorming

A brainstorming session needs to be well planned, and those who take part as group members need to be well briefed beforehand on how the sessions are to be conducted and on the rules they will be expected to apply. The brainstorming group should comprise 10–12 people: a leader, a scribe, and 8–10 regular and guest members. Ideally, it should take place away from the everyday place of work. The room needs comfortable chairs, flip charts, Blu-Tack, and marker pens.

There are a number of stages to brainstorming: a formal statement of the problem is given by the client; the brainstorming group then attempts to interpret the goals or objectives of the situation. A good technique for understanding goals is to use the 'how to' approach. For example, when looking for good new product ideas the problem might be variously defined as:

1 The client should be asked to state the problem and clarify any aspects which appear confusing to the group members.
2 The problem is recorded along with any redefinitions produced by the group.
3 The client picks the most useful redefinitions, which are then used for idea generation.
4 Ideas are then generated.

Problem taken:
   How to identify new profitable uses for a carton?
   Ideation stage:

- shoe boxes boards for notices
- folders videocassette and tape box
- components for picture frames egg holder
- advertising material envelopes

- hardware packaging wrapping material
- pencil cases chocolate packaging
- theatre stage décor perfume box
- dress models paper bin
- drawing and painting pads desk organiser

Round-robin brainstorming

Here again the rules are the same as those for classical brainstorming but, instead of the participants being encouraged to shout out ideas at random, each person in turn is asked to make a contribution. The 'round' is repeated several times until it appears that ideas have dried up or until a fixed period of time has elapsed.

Lateral thinking

Lateral thinking is about moving sideways when working on a problem to try different perceptions, different concepts, and different points of entry. The term covers a variety of methods, including provocations to get us out of the usual line of thought. Lateral thinking is cutting across patterns in a self-organising system, and has very much to do with perception. The term 'lateral thinking' can be used in two senses:

- Specific: a set of systematic techniques used for changing concepts and perceptions, and generating new ones
- General: exploring multiple possibilities and approaches instead of pursuing a single approach

Lateral thinking is a way of thinking that requires people to look at things in an unconventional manner and requires them to be aware of the limitations of their normal frame of reference. Three major activities go into making up lateral thinking:

1. Awareness
2. Alternatives
3. Provocative methods

Awareness

Here the concern is to redefine and clarify current ideas. It is argued that, before old ideas can be discarded or new ones adopted, current ones must be fully appreciated in terms of their good points and limitations. Current ideas can be examined from five different perspectives.

Dominant idea

Whether we like it or not, we are likely to have predispositions or dominant thoughts and ideas about a problem when we first approach it. We have to take steps to recognise the dominant ideas in our mind so as not to limit the scope of the kind of solutions to the problem which we will entertain. Knowing one-self and one's biases, attitudes, values, and expectations is very important, for they influence one's perception of problems and the factors relating to them.

For instance, if we are looking at why the firm's products are not as profitable as they might be, and the dominant idea in our mind is cost, then it is quite possible that we may overlook or pay insufficient attention to the other factors which influence profitability. Encouraging other people to give us their perspectives on a problem can be extremely helpful, for they may see things as being important which we have marginalised in our own mind. The *dominant idea* bias is similar to *mindset* explored in Chapter 2 and also to *perceptual blocks*, which were discussed in the same chapter.

Tethering factors

Tethering factors are really assumptions; that is, factors that are assumed to be included in the problem and which are overlooked. If the fire alarm sounds from time to time, and we come to learn that it is just a false alarm or simply random testing of the alarm, we come to believe that this is always the case. When a real emergency occurs, we may not respond as quickly as we should to the alarm. We need to be very much aware of these tethering factors so that we are not caught out because of them.

Polarising tendencies

This is reflected in an 'either/or' situation. Emotions may run high when a problem arises which involves the contrasting perspectives of individuals or groups of people. The emotions may lead to a polarising situation where neither party wants to step down from the way in which it views matters. Such a situation, of course, vastly reduces the number of possible solutions to such problems. Compromise is the order of the day.

Boundaries

The boundaries we put around a problem limit the amount of space that is available to solve it. Some problems may not be capable of a solution unless we look beyond the currently defined boundaries. At the very best, the solutions put forward may only be variations on old ideas, and these may not function too well.

Assumptions

We have already given attention to assumptions under the heading of *tethering factors*. However, it is important to repeat it here. All ideas relating to the solution of a problem make use of assumptions. We need to be aware of the assumptions we are making when we are looking for solutions to problems since the assumptions will limit the number of possible solutions that we can consider. If we assume, for example, that, while wood will float on water, metals such as iron and steel will not float on water under any circumstances, we might naturally only think of building sea-going vessels out of wood and not out of metal. New insights into problems can often be made by challenging basic assumptions.

Assumption smashing

A useful technique for generating ideas is to list the assumptions of the problem, and then explore what happens as you drop each of these assumptions individually or in combination.

Alternatives

This is concerned with searching for as many different ways of looking at a problem as possible. Different perspectives provide different insights into the problem.

Avoidance devices

Avoidance devices consist of developing a frame of mind in which one tends to ignore old ideas and be open to new ways of looking at things. The essence of this approach is summarised in the well-known saying 'Prevention is better than cure.'

Rotation of attention

Rotation of attention involves moving away from the core of the problem and shifting focus to the surrounding factors. It is natural to focus attention on the core of a problem, but this may not lead to creating new ideas. An example of rotation would be that, if the core of the problem seemed to be reducing manufacturing costs, another aspect of such a problem might relate to staffing costs or administrative costs.

Change of entry point

The *change of entry point* is a method which entails identifying the starting point for viewing the problem. People think in sequence; therefore by changing the point at which that sequence is started, different outcomes can be achieved. For example, the problem may concern improving the viewing figures for a television network. Initially, the problem might be redefined in terms of there being insufficient funds invested in its programmes. Another starting-point, however, would be to consider a more effective way of scheduling its programmes.

Quota of alternatives

Setting a *quota of alternatives* involves keeping only a few decidedly different options for consideration. This makes it easier to distinguish between ideas which may have too much in common and make it difficult to appreciate their fundamental differences.

Concept changing and challenging

Concept changing aims to prevent a problem being viewed from a fixed point. A barge, for example, might equally be considered as a mobile home or a holiday vehicle.

Concept challenging involves considering in depth any important statement usually taken for granted and challenging it in all ways possible. This assists with the suspension of judgement and helps one to escape from habitual thinking patterns.

The idea is to think of ways of communicating with business contacts without the aid of a telephone. Challenging a concept usually taken for granted can lead to questions such as 'Why does a product have to have certain properties or be made of a certain material, or be formed in a particular shape? For example, why do cars have to have doors on each side?' Another concept challenge might be 'Why does a company need a marketing manager?'

Provocative methods of lateral thinking

In order to gain insights into a problem de Bono (1970, 1971) advocates the use of a number of ideation techniques. Some of these are discussed below.

Cross-fertilisation

Here stimulation for an idea is provided by people working in different jobs or having different skills. One simply invites someone who is an expert in their field to say how they would approach a problem on which one is working – using the skill and knowledge they have achieved in their own field.

Recent developments in microsurgery have involved controlling the movement of instruments via movement simulation on a computer screen. In this case expert players at virtual reality computer games might be able to provide some assistance to surgeons regarding how to control movements on the computer screen with the aid of computer input devices such as joysticks, keyboards, mice, etc.

Problem switching

Insights which we gain from working on one problem may well give rise to new insights into another. The method advocates switching from one problem to another – or even interspersing problem solving with other activities – in the belief that this will enable new insights to be obtained. Interestingly, the method and the theory behind it have something in common with Graham Wallas's ideas about incubation.

Reversals

Reversals suggests that one should take a problem or a threat and seek various ways of refocusing so that the threat becomes an opportunity. The method:

- State the problem
- Make the statement negative: for example, if you are dealing with customer service issues list all the ways you could make customer service bad
- Doing what everybody else doesn't: for example, Apple Computers did what IBM didn't, Japan made small, fuel-efficient cars – something the Americans wouldn't consider at the time

Six Thinking Hats

The Six Thinking Hats method (de Bono, 1985) is a way to 'try on' different viewpoints. This can be very useful as a planning activity. Below is an outline that explains how to incorporate a critical thinking activity into the planning process.

The technique involves people working on a problem in a group and each member of the group adopting a different viewpoint or modes of thinking about the problem. A variety of hats are used to represent the different types of thinking as outlined below. These may be made or cut out of different coloured paper. Each hat is a different colour and represents a different type of thinking. The key is to have a visual that represents the different types of thinking. The group needs a facilitator, or at least someone who can collect thoughts and ideas that are generated during ensuing discussions.

Procedure

1 The group of six has to be provided with six different thinking hats. The six styles of thinking should be written down on a sheet of paper or a card and should be placed on each group's table as a reference. Each group member should be asked to familiarise themselves with each type of thinking.
2 Each one of the group should then select a hat or type of thinking. Having donned a hat (either literally or figuratively) they should then be asked to discuss the problem from the thinking viewpoint of the hat they have chosen.
3 Hats may be exchanged during the session to facilitate role changes or thinking approaches of group members.
4 Making use of what is contributed by group members one should then try to develop a solution for the problem.

Questions

1 What are the principles that lie behind morphological analysis? Illustrate how you might use the technique on a problem of your choice.
2 How would you use a checklist to find improvements for the following products?
   a) hair rollers
   b) washing powder (clothes)
   c) shoes
   d) new edition of a textbook
3 Suggest how you might use attribute listing to find improvements for the following:
   a) desktop computer
   b) wedding
   c) funeral
   d) checking in at an airport
   e) fun fair.
4 A department is experiencing problems with getting some of its members to participate fully in departmental activities. How might brainstorming be used to come up with possible solutions to such a problem? Illustrate your answer.
5 Brainstorming generates many useless ideas. To what extent would you agree with this statement? Explain.

6 Lateral thinking is more than a set of creative problem solving techniques. Discuss.
7 How does the Six Thinking Hats approach assist in the process of creative problem solving?

References

Allen, M.S. (1962) *Morphological Creativity*, Englewood Cliffs, NJ: Prentice Hall.
de Bono, E. (1970, 1971) *Lateral Thinking for Management*, New York: McGraw-Hill (republished in Pelican).
Eberle, B. (1996) *Scamper: Games for Imagination Development*, Austin, Tx: Prufrock Press Inc.
Osborn, A. (1957) *Applied Imagination: Principles and Procedures of Creative Thinking*, New York: Scribner.
Parnes, S.J. (1963) 'The deferment of judgement principle: a clarification of the literature', *Psychological Reports*, 12, 521–522.
Zwicky, F. (1948) *Discovery, Invention, Research through the Morphological Approach*, New York: Macmillan.

Further reading

Brown, V.R. and Paulus, P.B. (2002) 'Making group brainstorming more effective: recommendations from an associative memory perspective', *Current Directions in Psychological Science*, 11(6), 208–212.
Furnham, A. (2000) 'The brainstorming myth', *Business Strategy Review*, 11(4), 21–28.
Serrat, O. (2010) *Wearing Six Thinking Hats*, Washington, DC: Asian Development Bank.
Sloane, P. (2003) *The Leader's Guide to Lateral Thinking Skills: Powerful Problem-solving Techniques to Ignite Your Team's Potential*, London: Kogan Page.

7 Idea generating (analogical)

Introduction

In this chapter we will be examining the use of analogies and metaphors as aids to stimulating ideas. The techniques in this chapter are best suited to use when looking to stretch an existing paradigm or to break the existing one. The techniques covered are synectics, story writing, free association, and attribute association chains. Aspects of synectics are explored in some detail. The use of these methods is most useful when applied in a group creative problem solving session when people with a variety of thinking styles are present. Not only are divergent thinkers required but also those who can produce practical suggestions based upon the less practical ones that may be generated. Essentially, this means that an experienced facilitator would be helpful in leading such sessions.

Synectics

Synectics was developed by William J. Gordon (see Gordon, 1961). Like brainstorming it is a complete problem solving process and is particularly useful for problem identification and idea development. Synectics encourages the use of analogies (operational mechanisms) to make the familiar strange: through using personal, direct, symbolic, and fantasy analogies. It takes place with a group of people and a facilitator. We will first outline the stages in the process.

Stages of the synectics process

There are eight stages, as follows:

1 Problem as given
    A general statement of the problem is read to the group.

2 Short analysis of the problem as given

The main purpose of this stage is to make the familiar strange and then the strange familiar. This can be achieved in a number of ways: for example, the group can make use of metaphors and analogies. This may in fact generate satisfactory insights or even solutions into the problem. We will look at these operational mechanisms later in the chapter.

3 Purge

Here we eliminate rigid and superficial solutions suggested in the first two stages. This also can help to clarify the problem statement. The next step is called the 'purge.' When people hear of a problem they think of solutions. This is an opportunity to suggest them. These will be referred to the problem owner/poser for evaluation. Quite often it is something he or she may have tried and she or he will be asked to explain what happened and why it did not work.

4 Problem as understood

This stage begins with a selection of a part of a problem to work on. Each participant describes how he or she sees the problem. The facilitator then writes down each of these viewpoints. One is chosen in conjunction with the problem owner for further analysis.

5 Excursion

This part of the process may be viewed as an artificial vacation or holiday from the problem. It is during this stage that the operational mechanisms may also be used. The facilitator asks questions that will require or evoke an analogical answer. Following the generation of a number of analogies, the facilitator might then select one for more detailed analysis and elaboration.

6 Fantasy force-fit

Here the group has to work with the problem and the analogies until a new way of looking at the problem is found.

7 Practical force-fit

At this stage a practical application of the analogy developed at the previous stage is made.

8 Viewpoint or new problem as understood

The synectics process has to end with the production of a viewpoint (a way of looking at the problem). Once a viewpoint is selected, guidance needs to be provided to transform the viewpoint into a solution to the problem.

In summary, there are three major parts:

Defining and analysing the problem
Increasing understanding or making the familiar strange and vice versa
Integrating the results of using the operational mechanisms with the problem

Operational mechanisms

Personal analogy

Personal analogy is the use of emotions and feelings to identify an individual with the subject of a problem.

The problem may be how to vary a food product such as a fish finger. It may feel pain, be boring and may have a fishy odour which may not appeal to people. This may lead to some new element such as a tomato sauce filling being added to the product to negate the undesirable characteristics.

Personal analogy can involve:

a) Describing the object by listing its basic characteristics and relating these to the problem
b) Describing the emotions the object might have in a given situation
c) Describing how someone feels when using the object
d) Describing what it feels like to be the given object

Based upon such an approach, it might then be possible to develop solutions to the problem.

Example

Imagine that the problem is 'how to market a new perfume.' The personal analogy could be to imagine what it feels like to be 'the new perfume,' Some suggested feelings might be:

'I feel excited'
'I feel alluring'

Alternatively, of course, we could consider the characteristics of the perfume – fresh, long-lasting, etc.; the emotions that the perfume might have in given situations, etc. – sensitive to others at dinner, gay and joyful at parties; or what one might feel like when using the perfume – sophisticated, exciting, modern, playful, etc.

We might then look at ways of how we could try to incorporate these feelings into the promotion of the product (or, where negative, compensate for them in our promotional messages!). It is through such a technique that we are able to release ourselves from looking at a problem in terms of its previously analysed elements.

Characteristics

Fresh and long-lasting

Emotions

Sensitive to others at dinner, gay and joyful at parties

Feeling when using

Sophisticated, exciting, modern, playful

Object feelings

Excited, alluring

Direct analogy

The direct analogy compares the problem with homogeneous facts, information, or technology. A heating system might be compared with a volcano, and from this, new ideas may arise. A direct analogy is a mechanism by which we try to make comparisons with analogous facts, information, or technology. In making use of this device, we have to search our experiences and knowledge to collect phenomena that seem to exhibit similar relationships to those in the problem in hand. It is often fruitful to compare animate systems with inanimate systems, or to make comparisons between biological, ecological, and other natural science systems and social systems.

Example

Decision-making can be likened to finding one's way across paths over a marsh. There are many pitfalls and wrong turnings along the way. The various paths have different pay-offs, so we need to estimate the value of the various pay-offs. Will they enable us to reach our destination or objective?

The idea is to describe a clear, straightforward relationship between the problem and some object, thing, or idea with the expectation of being able to transfer insights back to the problem in hand. In this instance:

What are seemingly paths across the marshes often lead you the wrong way.

Transfers back to:

Unfamiliar and potentially hazardous options need careful prior analysis when making decisions in order to avoid mistakes.

Symbolic analogy

Symbolic analogy is the use of objective and personal images.

If the problem is to fit 50 people into a small conference room, it may be likened to cramming sardines into a can or the London Underground. Symbolic analogy involves making use of objective and personal images to describe a problem (e.g. like an Indian rope trick, like a thief in the night, like a pirate).

Example

It may be difficult to get hold of the boss because the boss is nearly always out of the office. Finding the boss may be likened to finding the elusive Scarlet Pimpernel. It might well be that in trying to suggest ways of finding the elusive flower (or fictional character of Baroness Orczy, who shares the same name) we may get some further insights into how to keep tabs on the whereabouts of the boss.

Getting hold of the boss is like finding the Scarlet Pimpernel. 'We seek her here, we seek her there, we seek her everywhere!'

Finding the flower might take account of the fact that it was once found in cornfields, but is now in decline due to intensive agricultural practices. It can still be found in arable fields, on roadside verges and waste ground, and on coastal cliffs. Can one find equivalent places in or outside of the organisation where the 'boss' might be found? For instance:

Arable fields – drumming up business, sorting out important matters
Roadside verges – travelling on business
Waste ground – sorting out routine problems
Coastal cliffs – firefighting
Who might know? – diary, personal assistant
Solution – an electronic diary on an intranet available for all to see. Who
    might know?

Fantasy analogy

This is based on Freud's notion that creative thinking and wish fulfilment are strongly related. It is usually prefaced by the words 'How do we in our wildest fantasy ...' For example, when considering a problem dealing with needing to introduce but at the same time disguise price rises, permanent or temporary, by making it appear that no price rise is in fact occurring. This might lead to such ideas as:

1   The discount structure can be altered so that the total profit to the company is increased, but the list price to customers remains the same.

2 The minimum order size is increased so that small orders are eliminated and overall costs thereby reduced.
3 Delivery and special services are charged for.
4 Invoices are raised for repairs on purchased equipment.
5 Charge for engineering, installation, and supervision.
6 Interest is collected on overdue accounts.

Excursions

Various types of excursion are used in the synectics process. The choice of excursion depends on the degree of novelty required in a solution, the element of risk the leader is prepared to take and the type of material which is being worked upon. Hicks (1991) distinguishes between 'imaging or fantasy excursion' and 'example excursion.' The imaging excursion is possibly the most unorthodox form of excursion and can be a potential disaster with a conservative-minded group – though it often works dramatically well when it is least expected and produces the most innovative ideas.

Fantasy excursion

For a fantasy or image excursion the group is asked to describe a mental picture/story inspired by the last item in a word-association preliminary exercise, starting with a word taken from the 'springboard.' One person will lead off, and then every other person in the group has to add to the story. They should be invited to jump in whenever they like and told that the more colourful, outlandish, weird, or exotic the story the better. It is usually better to keep the story in the same location, if possible, as this makes for better imagery. Everyone should try to add about a minute to the story, and then someone else takes over. The changeover may be left to the discretion of the leader.

If the story tends to stagnate on some minute detail of one particular image, the leader can ask someone to make something surprising happen. Conversely, if images are insufficiently developed because storytellers move too quickly to other images, the leader can pin people to one scenario by asking for more detail. People may be anxious about producing mental images in public and about their ability to contribute to the story. It is, however, the violent changing of direction and having to build another mental image after the destruction of the first that makes the story rich in speculation and evocative images.

Absurd solutions

When every group member has had at least one chance to contribute to the story the leader stops the imaging and asks the group to replay the story in their mind and try to think up some really absurd or impractical solutions to the problem. The absurd solutions are written up on the flip chart.

Having moved so far from the problem with the fantasy excursion, it usually becomes desirable to return to the real world and the problem in several stages, the first of which is this drawing up of absurd solutions. If a group member immediately comes up with a sensible and novel solution, one should obviously not reject it.

The leader needs to check with the problem owner to see if any of the absurd solutions intrigue, fascinate, or appeal to them. There should be no problem with picking too practical a solution as there should not be any. After the problem owner makes his or her selection the leader asks the group to examine the chosen absurd solutions and to try to find ways of changing them into something more practical and closer to reality, while retaining as much of the original idea as possible. It is better not to attempt to do this in one step but to spend some time modifying them, because there is a tendency to lose the novel feature contained in the absurd solution by jumping back to reality too quickly.

Example excursion (includes the use of analogies)

The example excursion is perhaps most commonly applied and easiest to interpret, though it is thought to be less generally applicable. It is introduced in the same general way as the fantasy excursion. When moving into the excursion we ask the group for examples of a keyword chosen from the problem restatements in a different 'world.' The choice of appropriate world is a matter of past experience and knowledge of those that seem to have worked well in the past. Almost any 'world' can be used – for example, sport, fashion, warfare, nature, physics, astrophysics, engineering and so on. Examples, of course, are only one form of analogy, and one can also ask for other forms of direct, personal, fantasy or symbolic analogy – see the examples of synectics in action in the next section. One often combines examples with some other form of analogy. All ideas are of course written up and eventually explored to see how they can provide insights into the problem under consideration.

Synectics in action

Fantasy excursion

A firm was looking for capital to invest in some risky ventures.

Problem statement: how to finance risky ventures

Word selected:	ventures
Word-association preliminary:	ventures, adventure, excitement, journey, aspiration, jungle, desert, joy

Weird story:

'Joy sat entrenched in the bob-sleigh. The ice seemed to seep up through the runners as it began to move. The speed gathered. The sun glinted on the mountains overlooking the course. The first corner came. All was safe. The angle steepened, and the speed increased. Joy's helmet touched the ice wall. A reverberation rang through her ears. Everything went out of focus except the track. It was white, fast, and steep. A big corner. Almost turned over. The finish in sight. Would she stop? Yes. Hugs and kisses. All over.'

Absurd solutions

1   Win the money on the races.
2   Give potential backers a ride on a bob-sleigh and charge them exorbitant fares for the ride.
3   Put on very risky bob-sleigh tournaments and charge spectators for the privilege of watching.
4   Produce all kinds of spectacular events which will have great entertainment value and will attract sponsorship and TV rights.

Practical solution

Make the ventures look very attractive propositions, stressing that what appears to be a risky venture will in fact be quite safe and have substantial pay-offs.

Example excursions

Two groups, on separate days, but under the direction of the same synectics leader, were assigned the task of finding insights into the problem of how to reduce stress at work. The following episodes occurred:

Group 1. Problem definition/redefinition:

_____
_____

How to reduce stress at work

How to work in a positive way
How to improve morale and reduce absenteeism
How to improve relations between staff

The word 'reduce' was chosen by the leader, and the group suggested the world of forestry for an excursion. The group was then asked to think of examples of using reduce in the world of forestry.

---

putting fires out
cutting paths through the forest
reducing tree disease
deforestation
cutting the undergrowth
stop illegal hunting of animals in the forest
removal of weeds

The leader then focused on animals being hunted in the forest and asked the group to imagine what it would be like to be an animal being hunted in the forest:

browned off	thinks it's game
scared	unfairness
premature death	pain, misery, suffering
looking for relatives that have been killed	trying to find somewhere to hide
running all the time	revenge
feeling it never stops	victimised
	(relentless pursuit)

Group 2. Problem definition/redefinition:

How to reduce stress in the workplace   How to work in a more peaceful company

How to make work pleasurable   How to reward good performance

---

The word 'pleasurable' was taken, and the suggested excursion was the family. Examples of pleasurable things in the context of the family generated by the group were:

home cooking	gatherings
support	family intimacy
cosiness	quarrelling
birthdays	storytelling at bedtime
family outings	sport (doing it together)
holidays	having meals together

The word 'gatherings' was then chosen for a further excursion, and the group was asked to give examples of the kind of emotions that might be encountered at a family gathering:

happiness	love
sadness	anger
satisfaction	togetherness
pride	belonging
frustration	boredom

Now you consider how the data might be used to give insights into the original problem.

Other techniques are discussed below.

Story writing

The technique, as the name suggests, involves writing a highly imaginative fictional story of, say, a few hundred words, and then relating it to the problem in hand. The story is then examined closely, and major principles, themes, expressions, thoughts, objects, etc., are listed separately. A long story can of course take considerable time to analyse for its relevance to a problem. On the other hand, of course, a very short story may not be rich enough in ideas to stimulate thought with respect to the problem under consideration.

The routine may be carried out in various ways. One such approach is the round-robin story and involves a group of people. Each member of the group contributes a line in the story-writing process. An alternative might be for one person to write the story, with the remainder of the group then working on its analysis and interpretation.

Example

Problem: How to win a big contract with a major supplier.

Story

The car pulled slowly onto the forecourt of the tall offices in Mayfair for the first visit. A doorman dressed in a smart uniform strode majestically to open the door, an umbrella in his hand. The lightning flashed and momentarily the building was silhouetted against the dark evening sky. A clap of thunder welcomed Hermione as she crossed the pools shimmering in the cool of the oncoming night air.

The steps seemed endless, the doors never-ending, computer screens still shining bright, as the clock approached 4.30 p.m. The Christmas decorations created a brightness and a warmth that disguised the underlying austerity. Young people chatting at their desks. Hermione smiled to herself – she too had been a junior office worker long ago.

A corner was turned and a large door was ajar. No sound issued from behind the door but in her mind, Hermione could hear the last-minute chatter of those whom she expected to meet. The door drew nearer, the pace slowed, one last thought on the opening gambit: should she stick to her guns throughout or be prepared to make all the concessions that had been asked for?

The next step involves picking out the relevant list of points from the story.

1 pulled slowly
2 first visit
3 tall offices
4 Mayfair
5 doorman dressed in a smart uniform strode majestically
6 umbrella
7 clap of thunder
8 pools shimmering in the cool of the oncoming night air
9 steps seemed endless
10 the doors never-ending
11 computer screens still shining bright
12 Christmas decorations creating a brightness and a warmth
13 underlying austerity
14 Hermione
15 she too had been a junior office worker
16 large door was ajar
17 chatter of those whom she expected to meet
18 the door drew nearer
19 the pace slowed
20 stick to her guns
21 prepared to make all the concessions

Next, we take the list of points raised and use them as a source of idea generation.

1 Take the process slowly and carefully – but not too slowly.
2 First stage in negotiations.
3 It is a tall order and needs a lot of consideration.
4 Likely to involve top level negotiation.
5 Look out for negotiators who seem important but who only play a minor role.
6 Contingency plans are always required.
7 Those who shout the loudest are likely to be effective.
8 Some things may look attractive but need to be on guard.
9 A long tiresome process – needs determination.
10 May be many people to see – time and time again.
11 People in the meeting are likely to be alert and on the ball.
12 Atmosphere may seem friendly … but underneath may not be.
13 It is very business-like.
14 Unusually sophisticated person required to conduct negotiations.
15 A person who now had a lot of business experience is now required.
16 The opportunity was waiting to be seized.
17 Those with whom she would meet would be well prepared.
18 Keep an open mind towards the end of the session.
19 Be deliberate during the final stages of first negotiations.
20 Do not make major concessions at this stage.
21 Possibly be prepared to go along with minor concessions.

Hermione eventually succeeded in making a deal after two further meetings. She agreed to two minor concessions and one major one. Her employers were satisfied with the terms of the contract, but within two years they terminated the contract and found new suppliers. In the meanwhile, Hermione had left the firm six months after agreeing the contract to take up a new job in a larger organisation at a substantial increase in salary.

Free association

Of all the idea-generating techniques this is one of the simplest. One idea is used to generate another, which is then used to produce a third, and so on. There are two forms of free association:

● Unstructured free association
   Here ideas are listed as they naturally occur and where one idea then leads to another. It is very similar to classical brainstorming.

- Structured free association

  Here the procedure adopted attempts to increase the relevance of ideas to a problem. The procedure adopted is as follows:

  1 A symbol – word, number, object, condition – that is directly related to the problem is drawn or otherwise recorded.
  2 Whatever is suggested by the first step, whether or not it seems relevant to the problem, is recorded.
  3 Step 2 is repeated until all possible associations have been listed.
  4 Associations that seem most relevant to the problem are selected from the list.
  5 The associations selected at Stage 4 are used to develop and produce ideas that appear capable of solving the problem. If the first effort does not produce useful insights then it is repeated using another symbol as the starting point – i.e. one recommences at Stage 1.

Example

A hotel wants to improve the facilities and services it offers to holidaying guests and is looking for ideas. It uses structured free association in the following way to gain new insights.

1 Stimulus word: history.
2–3 Thoughts recorded: visits to local museums and art galleries tours of local historical sites films and videos about local history library of books and documents on history round about antiques and collectors' fairs displays.
  4 Antiques/collectors fairs and displays.
  5 Hold weekly antique/collectors' fairs for the benefit of the paying guests and outsiders. Also mount permanent displays of antique/collectors' items which might be of interest to visitors.

Attribute association chains

Attribute association chains (Taylor, 1961) generate ideas by developing analogies for each of the major problem attributes. The procedure is as follows:

1 The major problem attributes are listed.
2 Sub-attributes for each major attribute are listed.
3 Look at one of the sub-attributes and write down the first word suggested.
4 Using this word as a stimulus, list the next word suggested and so on until four or five associations have been created.

5 Repeat Steps 3 and 4.
6 Using the free associations as stimuli, record any new ideas.

As an example, consider the problem of improving a car tyre. First, we write down the attribute and then the sub-attribute in each case.

Attribute. Sub-attribute
Name. Car tyre
Parts. Wall, tread, valve
Material. Rubber, air, metal
Function. Allow cars to run smoothly on roads
Next step, freely associate, using several of the attributes
Car tyre. Sponge, revolves, punctures, inflates
Valve. Central heating, canal lock, hot air balloon
Wall. Strong, keeps things out, castle, ladders
Tread. Softly, walk, slip, hike, hills, grip, deep
Rubber. Flexible, eraser, wellingtons, waterproof, synthetic
Air. Cushion of air
Metal. Suspension bridge, metal, Forth bridge
Smooth. Billiard table
Finally, use the free associations to stimulate ideas, for example, non-slip tyres for wet weather, toughened walls and tread to resist punctures, non-squeal tyres to reduce noise pollution.

Questions

1 A firm is having problems in recruiting new managers to join its ranks. Discuss how the use of free association might lead to ideas on how to get to grips with this problem.
2 What is synectics? Illustrate its application to a problem of your choice.
3 When might storytelling be most appropriately used in creative problem solving?
4 Illustrate the different forms of analogy that might be used in a synectics session (i.e. personal, direct, symbolic and fantasy analogy).
5 What is the purpose of an excursion? Suggest 'excursions' and an example of the following italicised keywords, in the excursions in each of the cases below:
   a) How to ignite *enthusiasm* for a project
   b) How to liquidate *assets* to solve a financial problem
   c) How to *purify* the air in departmental meetings

6 Work through a synectics session to gain insights into each of the following problems:

  a) How to improve communications between management and workers
  b) How to prevent industrial espionage
  c) How to minimise the number of industrial accidents
  d) How to do more management work with fewer resources

References

Gordon, W.J. (1961) *Synectics*, New York: Harper & Row.

Hicks, M.J. (1991) *Problem Solving in Business and Management*, London: Chapman & Hall.

Prince, G. (1970) *The Practice of Creativity: A Manual for Dynamic Group Problem Solving*, New York: Collier Books.

Taylor, J.W. (1961) *How to Create Ideas*, Englewood Cliffs, NJ: Prentice Hall.

Further reading

Faulkner, D. (2011) 'Angels, tooth fairies and ghosts: thinking creatively in an early years classroom', in Faulkner, Dorothy and Coates, Elizabeth (eds), *Exploring Children's Creative Narratives*, Abingdon: Routledge, 39–62.

Gassmann, O. and Zeschky, M. (2008) 'Opening up the solution space: the role of analogical thinking for breakthrough product innovation', *Creativity and Innovation Management*, 17(2), 97–106.

Nolan, V. (2003) 'Whatever happened to synectics?', *Creativity and Innovation Management*, 12(1), 24–27.

Proctor, T. (1989) 'The use of metaphors to aid the process of creative problem solving', *Personnel Review*, 18(4), 33–42.

Proctor, T. (2020) 'Creative problem solving techniques, paradigm shift and team performance', *Team Performance*, 26(7/8), 451–466.

8　Evaluation

Introduction

Having covered the methods of ideation in the previous chapters we now move on to looking at how we might evaluate ideas – assessing whether or not it is worthwhile taking any ideas that have been generated any further forward. Methods of evaluation range from simple checklists to complex weighted scoring systems. First, however, we look at sorting methods, and before turning to look at evaluation methods. Many of the ideation methods we have examined in the previous chapters produce a large quantity of ideas. Before we can evaluate these ideas, we need to sort them into categories or themes. This facilitates the process of making comparisons and evaluations. Finally, we give some thought to exercising choice. We look at a number of methods: advantage–disadvantage tables; plus, minus, interesting (PMI); castle technique; sticking dots; creative evaluation; weighting systems; reverse brainstorming; financial evaluation; mathematical evaluations; pay-off tables; and decision trees. We also look at strategic framing. While decision-making is important in this context we still have to consider the question of how decisions are implemented and this is the topic of the next chapter.

The following methods may be used to evaluate all the ideas that have been generated along a particular theme or grouping, or to evaluate/eliminate particular themes or groupings.

Creative evaluation

This also is a method which is useful for dealing with a large number of ideas. It attempts to present ideas in a format that will reduce the amount of time required for evaluation. All ideas are evaluated in terms of time and financial requirements. The procedure is as follows:

1 List the ideas.
2 Categorise the ideas into simple, hard, and difficult. Note that simple ideas are those which can be put into action with a minimum of expenditure of time and money. Hard ideas require more expenditure, while difficult ideas require the most expenditure.

Like the advantages–disadvantages method, this approach is most suitable for a cursory examination of a large number of ideas.

Culling, rating, and scoring screens

Culling screens

Criteria are developed that can be answered with a 'yes' or 'no' response. Ideas receiving a 'no' response to any of the culling criteria are eliminated.

Rating screens

Criteria are developed that can be answered with a 'yes' or 'no' response. Each 'yes' scores 1, each 'no' 0. A minimal passing score is established for the set of criteria. An idea falling below the minimum score for writing criteria is eliminated.

Scoring screens

Criteria are developed that can be answered with a rating response such as poor (1), fair (2), or good (3). Each criterion also receives a weighting – the more important the criterion, the greater the weighting. Each idea is rated against each criterion and a weighted score assigned for each criterion it is rated against. The totals of the weighted criterion scores are then summed. A minimal passing score is established for the set of criteria. An idea falling below the minimum score for rating criteria is eliminated (see Table 8.1).

Table 8.1 Scoring screen

Criterion	Poor	Fair	Good	Weight	Total
A	x	x	3	2	6 (3 × 2)
B	x	2	x	3	6 (2 × 3)
C	1	x	x	3	3 (1 × 3)
Minimum score is 17					15 (REJECT)

Advantage–disadvantage tables

Perhaps the simplest method of evaluating ideas makes use of tables which permit the comparison of the advantages and disadvantages of various ideas. For example, suppose there are two ideas about how we should reorganise the office – method A and method B. First, we list the criteria against which we want to compare and evaluate the ideas. The same criteria are used for both of the options, and space is left to indicate whether the idea was rated as having predominantly advantages or disadvantages when considered against those criteria.

The technique is useful as a rough evaluation tool, and in the example in Table 8.1 it will be noted that method B seems to have the better rating. However, except for possible use as a preliminary screening device, this approach has too many limitations. Its main weakness is of course that it assumes that all the criteria carry equal weight and that it is the overall score that is important (it overlooks the fact that some of the criteria may be critical – i.e. they must be satisfied).

More elaborate screening methods have been suggested by Hamilton (1974). The methods involve 'culling' ideas which fail to satisfy key criteria, and rating and scoring ideas against desirable criteria.

	Options			
	Method A		Method B	
Criteria	Advantage	Disadvantage	Advantage	Disadvantage
Efficiency	x		x	
Cost		x	x	
Employee satisfaction	x		x	
Score	2	1	3	0

Figure 8.1 Advantage–disadvantage method

PMI: plus/minus/interesting

PMI stands for 'plus/minus/interesting.' It is a development (by Edward de Bono) of the 'pros and cons' technique used for centuries.

One simply draws up a table headed 'Plus,' 'Minus,' and 'Interesting.' In the column underneath the 'Plus' heading one writes down all the positive points of taking the action. Underneath the 'Minus' heading one writes down all the negative effects. In the 'Interesting' column one writes down the extended implications of taking the action, whether positive or negative.

Castle technique

The castle technique is useful for evaluating a large number of ideas and is made up of four steps:

1 A time-limit for the exercise should be set – say, 1 hour.
2 Three criteria are used to evaluate each idea: acceptability (the extent to which it leads to a satisfactory solution), practicality (the extent to which it satisfies financial and time constraints), and originality (the extent to which it makes a significant improvement on the status quo).
3 Each participant in the evaluation exercise has the same number of votes as there are ideas. Participants are instructed to vote for each idea with either a 'yes' or a 'no' vote. One vote per idea per individual is allowed.
4 The two ideas which receive the highest number of positive votes (number of 'yes' votes minus number of 'no' votes) are then combined into one idea.

Force-field analysis

This is a method used to get a whole view of all the forces for or against an idea. In effect this is a specialised method of weighing pros and cons. Force-field analysis allows you to look at all the forces for or against the plan. It helps you to plan or reduce the impact of the opposing forces, and strengthen and reinforce the supporting forces. To carry out a force-field analysis, take the following steps:

- List all forces for change in one column, and all forces against change in another column.
- Assign a score to each force, from 1 (weak) to 5 (strong).
- Draw a diagram showing the forces for and against, and the size of the forces (see Figure 8.2).

A FIRM WHICH IS GOING FOR GROWTH

FORCES FOR	+9	FORCES AGAINST	−9
MORE SALES	+3	LOSS OF CONTROL BY EXISTING MANAGEMENT	−5
MORE PROFIT	+3		
MORE WORK FOR EMPLOYEES	+3	UNCERTAINTY	−4

Figure 8.2 Force-field analysis

Once you have carried out an analysis, you can assess the viability of the idea. Here you have two choices:

- to reduce the strength of the forces opposing a project
- to increase the forces pushing a project

Often the most elegant solution is the first: just trying to force change through may cause its own problems (e.g. staff can be annoyed into active opposition to a plan instead of merely not welcoming it).

If you were faced with the task of pushing through the project in the example above, the analysis might suggest a number of points:

- By looking for a strategic alliance, loss of management control could be reduced (reduce the loss of management control by 2)
- Coping with uncertainty is necessary for business survival (new force in favour, +2)
- More work will mean a more productive workforce (new force, +1)
- More sales will increase the morale of sales force (new force, +1)
- More profit will increase the satisfaction of shareholders (new force, +1)

These changes swing the balance from 9:9 (neither for nor against the plan) to 14:7 (in favour of the plan).

Force-field analysis is an effective method of getting a picture of all the forces for and against a plan. It helps you to weigh the importance of these factors and to assess whether a plan is worth pursuing. Where you have decided to proceed with a plan, carrying out a force-field analysis helps you identify changes that might be made to improve the plan.

Qualitative evaluation

Reverse brainstorming

The technique was developed at the Hotpoint company (Whiting, 1958) as a group method for discussing all possible weaknesses of an idea, or what might go wrong with an idea when it is implemented. It is almost identical to classical brainstorming except that criticisms rather than ideas are generated.

Imagine the problem being how to counteract declining sales and that the following potential ideas for solutions were generated by classical brainstorming or some other ideation method:

new advertising strategy   change or improve packaging
offer discounts   find new markets

door-to-door sales

The first step in reverse brainstorming is to suggest criticisms for the first of these ideas – a new advertising strategy. Criticisms developed might be:

too expensive
unable to target the specific areas required

After exhausting criticisms for the first idea the group begins criticising the second idea, and the process continues until all the ideas have been criticised.

Using classical brainstorming the group then re-examines the ideas to generate possible solutions for each weakness that has been identified. For example, in the case of the second idea, 'offer discounts,' the criticisms might be that people might perceive the quality of the product not to be good as a result of offering discounts. In the case of 'door-to-door sales,' it might be the fact that unacceptable training and added costs will be incurred because of the need to employ more sales staff. Other criticisms will no doubt be found for the other ideas. As far as solutions to these criticisms are concerned, it may not be felt that there are any in, say, the case of a 'new advertising strategy'; however, in the case of 'door-to-door sales' it may be felt possible to employ part-time workers in order to lower the cost.

The idea that possesses the lowest number of weaknesses, and that will be most likely to solve the problem, is usually selected for implementation. Of course, one does also have to bear in mind the comparative seriousness of any unresolved criticisms.

Example

Problem: getting people to have a positive attitude towards adopting new ways of working.

Ideas:

1 Rewards associated with adopting new methods
2 Firing those who do not co-operate and hiring new staff
3 Training people and giving them the right kind of skills to do the new tasks

Criticisms:

1 May be too costly
   a) May not believe they will receive rewards, or seen as further manipulation by management
2 a) Will cause even more hostility and resentment
   b) Difficult to identify best method of recruitment – may still hire inappropriate people
   c) Effort and time need to be spent on recruitment and interviews
3 a) Training requires additional time and cost
   b) Not possible to provide training for every situation

Solutions to weaknesses:

1 a) Link the new methods with productivity increases
   b) Provide written agreements to show commitment.
2 a) No solution
   b) Agree that all new appointees be on probation for a fixed period.
   c) Hire recruitment consultants.
3 a) Provide training on the job.
   b) As (a), plus make sure first line managers can provide proper guidance and support to workers.

Although both ideas 1 and 3 seem to have resolved all the difficulties associated with them, 3 might well be the preferable alternative. This is because the problem at the core of the matter lies in a decrease in productivity which is incurred as each new method is adopted.

Disjointed incrementalism

Objectives in policy analysis are often poorly defined and constantly changing. Alternatives are not evaluated by establishing whether one of them is more useful than another. One simply asks whether a change in one of them is preferred to a change in another. So, for example, it is not asked whether strikes are preferred less than salary increases, but how much in terms of salaries could be sacrificed to avert strikes. The steps involved are:

1 Determine the consequences of the present state of the problem.
2 List the alternatives known or expected to be different from each other incrementally, and from the present state of the problem.

3 Rank in order the alternatives in terms of preference, according to the degree of incrementalism by which the alternatives differ.
4 Resolve conflicts between alternative preferences by stating how much one value is worth sacrificing to achieve an increment of another.

This kind of approach often leads to the alleviation of a problem rather than a resolution (Lindblom,1959).

Example

A firm is looking to recruit a new member to its research team. Experience shows that if it recruits a graduate aged 21–23 the person will still with the company for approximately two years before moving on elsewhere. On the other hand, if it recruits an experienced researcher with five or more years' experience, it can expect that the person will stay five years or more. The firm estimates that an experienced person will be 50 per cent more productive in terms of his or her contribution to the research of the firm, but to be competitive in the recruitment market it will have to pay a new graduate at a rate of at least two thirds of the average salary it pays to its experienced staff. The firm then has to constantly review its policy on recruiting new graduates and the salaries it pays its experienced staff.

Strategic framing

Organisations are guided by strategic visions and planning processes. When they decide to innovate, they create strategic innovation frames to guide the innovation process. A primary obstacle is how to state innovation challenges and link together objectives so they will produce strategic results.

Many innovation initiatives may fail because all of the secondary objectives were not detailed and linked together appropriately. An organisation may simultaneously be concerned about maintaining its image, improving cash flow, maintaining highly motivated managers, and keeping good relations with other staff and trade unions. These may all be corporate objectives and the overarching task is how to link them all together in the best manner. Complex, interrelated decisions such as these are associated with objectives that are nested within hierarchies of other, related objectives and multiple goals typically must be achieved to accomplish one primary goal.

The problem is to identify which objective or goal should be accomplished first to achieve the primary objective. It is also important to identify how the different objectives might be interdependent – that is, linked in ways so that achieving one will help achieve another.

Visual diagrams of strategic goals and objectives can be represented in cognitive maps. (For a comprehensive review of strategy, Van Gundy (2007) shows how the use of such diagrams and maps can help unravel the complexities of multiple goals and objectives when evaluating ideas.) Here we will discuss a simplified illustration of the concepts involved. Let us assume that the four objectives that the organisation is trying to satisfice are:

maintaining its image
improving cash flow
maintaining highly motivated managers, and
keeping good relations with other staff and trade unions

If we arrange the objectives in the form of a hierarchical cognitive map (Figure 8.3) we will see that improving the cash flow is seen as the prime objective but that maintaining the organisational image is a contributing factor to this. Any idea that does not satisfice in terms of enabling maintenance of the organisational image may not contribute to improving the cash flow. We say 'may not' rather than 'will not' because we cannot be absolutely certain of this. It could be that the firm can improve cash flow in the short term by issuing a notice of intention to customers that it will take legal redress where bills are not settled within 40 days. This may be seen

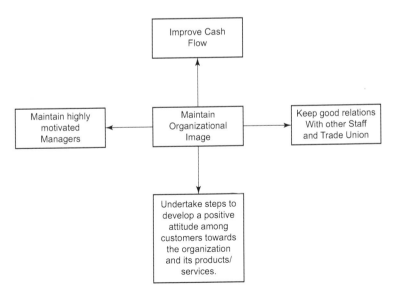

Figure 8.3 Cognitive mapping of the hierarchy of objectives and goals

as the mark of an efficient company with whom it should continue to deal by some customers but may be viewed as overly threatening by others. The net effect may be productive in the short term but may be less effective or even have a negative effect in the long run. In addition to customer attitudes towards the organisation, maintaining the organisational image is seen to be affected by motivation levels of managers and staff, too, so any idea should be seen to satisfice in this respect as well. A more elaborate cognitive map might take each of the boxes in the diagram and produce cognitive maps relating to each one. Ideas might then also be screened or evaluated against each of these to assess whether they are likely to satisfice on critical criteria.

Choosing an evaluation method

In this chapter we have considered a variety of techniques for evaluating ideas. These range from the very simple to the quite complex. When choosing an appropriate method, one should examine the advantages and disadvantages of each in relationship to the problem which is being studied so that an appropriate choice can be made. Thus while, for example, reverse brainstorming may seem an appealing method it may not be suitable for all kinds of problems. Indeed, it may be that more than one method may need to be applied. This is particularly the case where an evaluation by reverse brainstorming produces a number of attractive options, but where it is difficult to differentiate between their various appeals and to put them into some kind of rank order. Under such circumstances a rating procedure may be required to enable the various options to be ranked.

In other circumstances, of course, it may be possible to select from a range of options without having recourse to simple or elaborate evaluation models such as those we have outlined above. If this is the case, then one should not feel that it is a requirement that an evaluation model should be used.

Questions

1 Describe two different techniques which can be used to assist in the evaluation of ideas.
2 'Ideation techniques only generate insights into a problem and not solutions to a problem.' To what extent would you agree or disagree with this statement? How does this influence how we might set about the process of evaluating the output of an ideation process?
3 A manager has a number of proposals for improving communications in the office. How might he or she set about evaluating the different proposals?

4 When might one use reverse brainstorming? Describe the process.

5 What are the advantages of using reverse brainstorming compared with other methods of evaluation? What are its limitations? Illustrate its application to a situation of your own choice.

6 What is the purpose of reverse brainstorming? Illustrate its use through an example of your own choice.

7 A canning company is considering vertical integration as a means of obviating supply- and distribution-chain problems that have become apparent in the past few months. Discuss how force-field analysis might be used to good effect in helping to analyse such a situation.

References

Hamilton, H.R. (1974) 'Screening business development opportunities', *Business Horizons*, August, 13–34.

Lindblom, C.E. (1959) 'The science of "muddling through"', *Public Administration Review*, 19(2), 79–88.

Van Gundy, A.B. (2007) *Getting to Innovation: How Asking the Right Questions Generates the Great Ideas Your Company Needs*, American Management Association.

Whiting, C.S. (1958) *Creative Thinking*, New York: Van Nostrand Reinhold.

Further reading

Faure, C. (2004) 'Beyond brainstorming: effects of different group procedures on selection of ideas and satisfaction with the process', *The Journal of Creative Behavior*, 38, 13–34.

Licuanan, B.F., Dailey, L.R. and Mumford, M.D. (2007) 'Idea evaluation: error in evaluating highly original ideas', *The Journal of Creative Behavior*, 41(1), 1–27.

Puccio, G.J. and Cabra, J.F. (2012) 'Idea generation and idea evaluation: cognitive skills and deliberate practices', in M.D. Mumford (ed.), *Handbook of Organizational Creativity*, San Diego, CA: Elsevier, 189–215.

9   Implementing ideas

Introduction

In this chapter we examine some of the problems of implementing ideas. First, we consider the various sources of resistance to change. Next, we look at the role of communication in overcoming resistance to change. This is followed by an examination of how ideas might be put into action. Lastly, we look at how we might foster a climate for change in an organisation.

The successful introduction of new ideas helps maintain an effective organisation and sustain a competitive advantage in the marketplace. New ideas are not accepted automatically; they are often resisted. Knowing what resistance there will be is the first step in introducing change. Getting people to accept the need for new ideas through good communication is a key element in the process of effecting change. Various communication models are considered, along with identifying within an organisation spheres of influence needed to implement ideas and change. Contingency plans are necessary when implementing ideas. One needs to anticipate the problems that will arise and the objections that will be raised. The importance of 'potential problem analysis' as a technique that can be used to good effect in this latter context is considered in the chapter.

Ideas are not readily implemented

Getting new ideas off the ground can meet considerable opposition, and it is important to recognise this before embarking on introducing change into an organisation.

It is easy to imagine that throughout history the ideas of original inventors were sufficient to start off some new development. However, it is obvious on deeper reflection that the inventions themselves, as well as those who produced them, would be bound to fail if there was no need, demand, or social basis for the ideas. As a consequence, it is not surprising that many so-called inventions have been produced several times until eventually the time for their introduction has been appropriate. At the same time, developments in people's ways of life, new social orders influencing production and demand, have stimulated inventors to work along certain lines. It may not therefore have been pure chance that the railway and steam engines reached maturity at about the same time, and that they were brought together for the first time in England, the country, at the time, where social and economic developments were more rapid than anywhere else in the world. 'The locomotive is not the invention of one man,' said Robert Stephenson, 'but of a nation of mechanical engineers' (Larsen, 1961: 125).

Sources of resistance to change

There are many sources of resistance to change. Perhaps the most significant is that many people are afraid of new ideas. They may feel threatened by new ideas and fear that they will not be able to cope with a change in working patterns that is demanded of them or that they will not understand how to use a new technology. Even today there are many older people who are afraid of the desktop computer! Another point is that people may have a vested interest in not accepting change. Why change when you are doing very nicely with things as they are?

Resistance to change has many sources. Fear of the unknown, lack of information, threats to status, fear of failure, and lack of perceived benefits are examples of such sources. However, one of the most important sources is that people resist being treated as pawns in an organisational reshuffle. People like to feel that they are in control of what is happening to them, and the more that change is imposed from outside by others, the more they will see it as something to feel threatened about and the more they will resist it. People resort to using their last remaining powerbase: their will to co-operate.

People like to feel that they are in control of what is happening to them, and the more that change is imposed from outside by others, the more they will see it as something to feel threatened about and the more they will resist it.

Human and technological factors produce implementation blocks. While some of the blocks are intentional and are designed as checks to ensure that an organisation always functions smoothly, other blocks are unintentional and may arise from how the organisation has developed historically. It can be argued that organisations tend to stagnate as they age. A third type of block may arise from an outside source – a change in market demand, for example, can act as a barrier to idea implementation.

Blocks to implementing ideas and change reflect such things as a lack of adequate resources to implement ideas, a lack of commitment and motivation in those required to implement ideas, resistance to change, procedural obstacles, perceived risk associated with implementing ideas, political undercurrents, lack of co-operation in the organisation, and so on. The important thing is to uncover what resistance is likely to arise and what the reasons for the resistance are likely to be. With this information one can look for ways of implementing ideas so that the resistance encountered can be reduced.

Role of communication in overcoming resistance to change

The key to effecting change is to involve people in the process early, to consult them and to get them to take ownership for themselves of the new ideas that are to be introduced (see, for example, Coch and French, 1948). To sustain a programme of change it is essential to understand the culture of the organisation in which new ideas are to be introduced. New ideas that run counter to the traditional values of an organisation are the ones that are most difficult to introduce. Organisational culture is the pattern of shared values and norms that distinguishes it from all others (Higgins, 2005). Before one thinks about implementing change, one needs to create a readiness for change within an organisation. One needs to think of the organisation as an internal market for change initiatives where ideas have to be marketed. This means that opinions and attitudes have to be assessed and potential sources of resistance identified. Commitment to change can be instigated by helping people to develop a shared diagnosis of what is wrong in an organisation and what can and must be improved ().

Communication is the spearhead of ensuring that successful change can take place (see, for example, Higgins, 2005). It helps to overcome ambiguity and uncertainty, and provides information and power to those who are the subject of change. It enables them to have control over their destiny, to understand why change is necessary, and provides the suppressant to fear. Through open communication channels people can express their doubts about the effectiveness of proposed changes and can understand the necessity for new ideas. Relying on an attempt to implement ideas only from the top is likely to meet with difficulties. Grass-roots change is the only way to ensure that the process becomes firmly embedded. It is natural for people to resist change, and by anticipating, identifying, and welcoming resistance we convert resistance into a perceived need for change.

Putting ideas into practice

There are a variety of tools and techniques which can be used to good advantage in helping to introduce new ideas in a systematic and planned way into an organisation. 'Consensus mapping,' recommended by Hart *et al.* (1985), is one such tool. It helps those involved in the process of implementation to visualise, analyse, and organise ideas that are sequence dependent. In applying the technique, a graphic map is produced which portrays implementation steps and ideas in relationship to one another and shows how they are related to one another. *COPE* or *The Decision Explorer* is a computer package which can be used to achieve a similar goal. *PERT* networks and research-planning diagrams may also be used to good effect in facilitating the implementation of new ideas. Similarly, computer simulation methods can provide a basis for showing the impact new ideas will have on people and processes as well as on costs and efficiency. Another useful method, put forward by Kepner and Tregoe (1976), is 'potential problem analysis.' This method places an emphasis on a systematic approach to anticipating problems that are likely to stand in the way of the successful implementation of a project, changes, or ideas. Some of these methods are discussed in this chapter.

Besides the use of tools to systematise the introduction of new ideas there is also the task of persuading people who are going to make use of those ideas that they are worth using. Ideas may have to be sold to people who can authorise their implementation. This may make it easier to arouse subsequent motivation to implement ideas among those who have to do the job and make the chance of a successful implementation more likely. Putting ideas into practice usually requires:

1 An ability to get people to accept ideas
2 An ability to cope with difficult obstacles
3 An ability to plan and manage time in an effective manner
4 An ability to create the enthusiasm and motivation to follow through ideas

Persuading people to view new ideas in a favourable light when they are not readily disposed to do so essentially involves influencing and changing attitudes. To do this, it is first necessary to convince people that they need to be dissatisfied with the status quo. It is important to note that people may not readily recognise that they are dissatisfied with the current situation. One cannot assume that people will readily accept that a problem exists, even when it is blatantly obvious to an outsider. It may be necessary to:

1 Create an awareness of problems that exist and make people recognise that there is a need for change and a need to adopt the idea that is being put forward.

2 Point out to people the potential hazards and pitfalls of not accepting the need for change.
3 Stress the benefits of change to the individuals involved since they will only be motivated to accept and to adopt new ideas when they perceive and acknowledge that it is in their own best interest to do so.

Spheres of influence

We have to recognise that people are part of a group in the organisation. Getting people to change means getting the group to change and involves understanding the nature of group dynamics. Identifying opinion leaders, action initiators, people with status and influence in the group, and those most affected in carrying out the changes required is therefore very important. It is also important to have the backing of someone who has the authority and the resources to enable an idea to get off the ground. Knowing how to communicate with the target audiences is therefore an important skill when trying to implement new ideas and effect change.

Communication models

Communication theories offer several different descriptive models of the process by which it is thought that people adopt ideas as a result of receiving information about them. The models can also be used prescriptively as aids to producing communications that are intended to bring about action. One of the earliest models used was the AIDA model (origin uncertain). The model comprised four stages:

attracting ATTENTION;
maintaining INTEREST;
arousing DESIRE;
getting ACTION.

The early 1960s saw considerable interest in advertising models. Lavidge and Steiner (1961) developed the 'hierarchy of effects' model. This model was directly related to understanding how marketing communications worked. The model implied a six-stage process where the customer moves through stages from awareness to purchase:

AWARENESS → KNOWLEDGE → LIKING → PREFERENCE → CONVICTION → PURCHASE

Different persuasive activities were considered fitting to move customers through the various stages. To develop AWARENESS, teaser campaigns, sky writing, jingles, slogans, and classified advertisements are considered suitable. In order to convey KNOWLEDGE, announcements and descriptive copy were recommended. Image advertising and status or glamour appeals are envisaged to be ways of producing a LIKING, while competitive advertisements and argumentative copy are more relevant to generating a PREFERENCE. Finally, price appeals and testimonials may produce CONVICTION, while deals, last-chance offers, and point-of-purchase retail-store advertisements are seen as ways of encouraging actual PURCHASE.

Contemporary with Lavidge and Steiner, Colley (1961) produced a model called DAGMAR, which stands for defining advertising goals, measuring advertising results. It was argued that a communication must carry a prospect through four levels of understanding:

AWARENESS → COMPREHENSION → CONVICTION → ACTION

Shortly after, Rogers (1962) suggested the 'Innovation Adoption' model. In this case the theory was not directed specifically at the relationship between marketing communications and sales but rather at the adoption of a new idea. Several stages were suggested in the model:

AWARENESS → INTEREST → EVALUATION → TRIAL → ADOPTION

All of these models seem to fit in well with the more general communications model of:

EXPOSURE → RECEPTION → COGNITIVE RESPONSE → ATTITUDE
→ INTENTION → BEHAVIOUR

The point about all the above models is that attitude change and subsequent action are seen as a gradual step-by-step process. The models will be appropriate for different circumstances depending upon exactly what is required concerning the idea that is being implemented. Moreover, different ways of communicating, and even different communication media, may be more appropriate for moving people from one stage to the next.

Effective communications need to appeal to the needs and wants of the recipients. They should give the recipient a motive or incentive to act. They also need to generate involvement with the message on the part of the recipient by asking questions which leave the message incomplete. In addition, they should also explain exactly what course of action it is expected the recipient will follow.

Getting people to consider adopting an idea or changing behaviour can be achieved through appealing to their cognitive processes. One needs to arouse desire, indicate a need, or offer a logical reason why they should co-operate. In so doing the message becomes implanted in the recipient's memory and can be triggered by future needs, motives, and associations. However, one does have to remember that the rational approach may not be so effective for some recipients or in situations where there is likely to be less involvement in the action required. In these cases, emotional appeals may be used. The appeal, theme, idea, or unique selling proposition is what the communicator has to get over to the target audience to produce the desired response. Benefit, identification, motivation are all concepts that can be built into the message. Messages can be built around rational, emotional, or moral appeals, themes, ideas, or unique selling propositions. Economy, value, and performance are used in messages with a rational content. Emotional appeals make use of both positive and negative aspects. On the negative side this involves fear, guilt, and shame (Janis and Feshback, 1982), while on the positive side it comprises humour (Beggs, 1989), love, pride, and joy. Too much fear in a message may cause the audience to reject it. The use of humour may generate 'noise' and interfere with the message. Moral appeals address people's sense of what is right and just.

Reducing resistance to change

A good way to counter resistance to change is to pre-empt the possibility of it occurring. As is mentioned above, getting people involved in the idea-development process in the first place anticipates resistance to change. Resistance is reduced because people feel that they have had the opportunity to participate and express their view.

Getting people to change their attitudes is fundamental to reducing resistance to new ideas. While creating dissatisfaction with the status quo is one method of effecting attitude change and getting ideas implemented, there are other ways of achieving the same objective. A good way to counter resistance to change is to pre-empt the possibility of it occurring. Getting people involved in the idea-development process in the first place anticipates resistance to change. Resistance is reduced because people feel that they have had the opportunity to participate and express their view.

In the same way that attitude change is seen as a gradual process, the implementation process should follow a similar pattern. New ideas that involve substantial change need to be implemented gradually, smoothly, and systematically. Resistance to change can be softened by making the changes tentative rather than definite or permanent. It is a good strategy to get people to try out ideas initially for a short period. In addition, people should be encouraged to say whether they think an idea is working. If a new idea fails, it does not cause its originator as much loss of face under such circumstances.

Encouraging people to recognise that change is a normal facet of life is important. If they come to accept this viewpoint, they will not see change as being out of the ordinary when it is applied to them. It can help them to become less emotionally attached to the status quo.

In introducing a new idea, one has to be reasonably sure that it is worthwhile. There is a cost associated with change, for it causes disruption to those who are concerned. However, provided that the required change is accompanied by demonstrable benefits which more than offset the costs of disruption, the new idea is more likely to meet with little resistance. In addition, it will pave the way for the introduction of future new ideas in that it is more likely to be seen as in the interests of the organisation.

Potential problem analysis

Kepner and Tregoe (1976) developed potential problem analysis (PPA) to alleviate the risk of new problems occurring during the implementation of new ideas and processes. Eight steps were involved in PPA:

1 Determine exactly what should take place if the task is to be done successfully.
2 Employ *reverse brainstorming* to identify everything that can go wrong during implementation.
3 Detail highlighted problems.
4 Assess and evaluate the impact of each identified potential problem on the implementation of the whole project.
5 Look for causes of the identified new problems.
6 Assess the probability of occurrence of each one of the potential problems.
7 Determine ways of minimising the effect of the potential problems.
8 Develop contingency plans for the most serious potential problems.

PPA provides a systematic framework to help implementers of ideas avoid the occurrence of the events of Murphy's Law (Bloch, 1990). Murphy's Law states that if anything can go wrong it will. PPA also helps to get to grips with many of the possible corollaries to Murphy's Law. For example,

1 Nothing is as easy as it looks.
2 Everything takes longer than you think.
3 If there is a possibility of several things going wrong, the one that will cause the most damage will be the one to go wrong.
4 Left to themselves, things tend to go from bad to worse.

5 Whenever you set out to do something, something else must be done first.
6 Every solution breeds new problems.

Post-implementation

One has to make sure that what has been implemented actually works for more than just a couple of days and does not fall down because of something which has not been foreseen. That is not to say that there will not be complaints about what has been implemented. It is quite likely that the change agents or idea implementers will be inundated with messages, both from people who supported the new idea and from people who opposed it, saying that things do not seem to be working properly.

Feedback messages about new ideas that have been implemented may take the form of:

a) *Grousing.* This usually does not require action and simply reflects people's resistance to change. People may complain because they are required to do things in a different way.

b) *Errors of detail.* Aspects of detail may have been overlooked. When the detail is not critical it is usually possible to remedy the situation fairly easily. Elements that are critical to the functioning of the whole, however, are more problematic and may require thorough analysis and reflection. In some cases they may even temporarily hold up matters until they can be resolved.

c) *Apparently major errors.* These can be either real or supposed. In the latter case it is simply a matter of reassuring all concerned that it is only supposition. Where the problem is real, then the implementation of the whole project may be at risk.

Ideas and changes must be workable and reliable. Thinking through and testing out ideas before they are finally implemented is highlighted as a critical stage of the process.

Climate for change

Any organisation wanting to become more creative needs to be aware of the necessary conditions for creativity to thrive. Three prerequisites are:

1 The right climate
2 An effective system of communicating ideas
3 Procedures for managing innovation

A firm in which the climate is either hostile or indifferent to ideas is unlikely to be creative. But what is the right climate? First, the organisation must be prepared to finance creative ideas. It is also very important that top management should encourage creativity at all times. Negativity has to be avoided at all costs. If those at the top do not take creativity seriously, they send out messages to others in the organisation who will also tend to accept the same perspective. In an organisation without good communications, good ideas can be lost simply because people do not know whom to inform about their ideas.

Old behaviour and attitudes are often deeply embedded in the (comfortable) relationships which have been built up over the years. Any significant change generally suggests an upset or reshuffling of these relationships, and a change of one's position relative to others in the workplace. It appears that new thinking and new behaviour patterns are most readily and firmly established when they are conditions of regular membership in a new group, for group members exercise the most powerful tool for shaping behaviour.

Questions

1 A firm is trying to get its employees to participate in a new job-enlargement scheme. Indicate the difficulties that might be encountered when trying to implement such a scheme. Outline the mechanisms that can be used to help deal effectively with such problems.

2 An organisation is experiencing problems in implementing a new computer-based information system in its finance department. Illustrate how a cognitive mapping device might be used to help gain insights into this problem.

3 Discuss the problems encountered in implementing ideas and indicate the various ploys which can be used to help get around these problems.

4 Machiavelli wrote: 'there is nothing more difficult to take in hand, more powerless to conduct or more uncertain in its success than to take the lead in the introduction of a new order of things because the innovators have for enemies all those who would have done well under the old conditions and lukewarm defenders in those who may do well' (*The Prince*, ch. 5). Discuss the implications of Machiavelli's thinking for the implementation of ideas. What steps can be taken to try to circumvent some of the difficulties that might arise in the way that Machiavelli suggested?

5 A firm is trying to get its employees to change their operating procedures to improve efficiency in the workplace. What kind of difficulties might be encountered when trying to implement such a scheme? Indicate what you would do in order to deal effectively with such difficulties.

6   Getting good ideas adopted by management can often pose problems. Indicate the nature of the problems and outline the mechanisms that can be applied to overcome the difficulties presented by the problems.

References

Beggs, W.B. (1989) 'Humour in advertising', *Link*, 2, 15.

Bloch, A. (1990) *Murphy's Law Complete*, London: Mandarin.

Colley, R.H. (1961) *Defining Advertising Goals for Measuring Advertising Effectiveness*, New York: Association for National Advertising.

Hart, S., Borush, M., Enk, G. and Hornick, W. (1985) 'Managing complexity through consensus mapping: technology for the managing of group decisions', *Academy of Management Review*, 10(3), 587–600.

Higgins, J.M. (2005) *101 Creative Problem-Solving Techniques*, Winter Park, FL: New Management Pub. Co.; Revised edition.

Janis, I. (1982) *Groupthink: Psychological Studies of Policy Decision*, Boston, MA: Houghton Mifflin.

Kepner, C.H. and Tregoe, B.B. (1976) *The Rational Manager*, Princeton, NJ: Kepner-Tregoe.

Larsen, E. (1961) *A History of Invention*, London: Phoenix House.

Lavidge, R.J. and Steiner, G.A. (1961) 'A model for predictive measurements of advertising effectiveness', *Journal of Marketing*, October, 58–62.

Rogers, E. (1962) *Diffusion of Innovations*, New York: Free Press.

Further reading

Klein, K.J. and Knight, A.P. (2005) 'Innovation implementation: overcoming the challenge', *Current Directions in Psychological Science*, 14, 243–246.

10 Digital creativity

Introduction

In general, so far, computers have not been specifically harnessed to produce creative ideas and insights for managers by themselves. Rather it has been through the interaction of people and computers that ideas have been produced. There is now a range of computer software which can be used to assist creative problem solving. This stretches from purpose-built software to more general-purpose software which can be used to stimulate creative thinking. In addition, some software is useful for the individual working alone while other software is of benefit to groups of individuals working on a problem or project together. The amount of software available has expanded considerably over the past few years with recent development of applications which will run on hand-held and mini computers fitted with touch screens – commonly referred to as 'apps.' Developments on the internet have also led to the setting up of social network sites and these have facilitated the ideation process. Indeed, the very existence of information on internet sites can act as a spur to ideation. Photographs and videos can act as a spur to ideation and with the aid of computers their use can be made in creative problem solving sessions. Alongside the above, there have been developments in software that facilitate visualisation, Artificial Intelligence, and Big Data analysis.

History of development

Simon (1985) discussed a computer program called BACON, which he had developed with co-workers. He argued that if a computer program was able to make discoveries which, if made by a human, could be considered creative, then the processes it used should provide useful information about the creative process. The BACON programme received raw observational or experimental data and produced, when successful, scientific laws. Simon wanted to show that scientific discovery is an understandable phenomenon which can be explained in terms of all the same kinds of basic information-processing mechanisms that account for other forms of human problem solving and thinking. Simon's efforts were directed at getting a computer to undertake creative problem solving by itself.

Computer-aided creative-thinking and problem solving mechanisms began to appear in the late 1970s. Rokeach (1979) put together a computer program which enabled individuals to examine their own value systems and clarify their knowledge. Planet (designed by Shaw, 1982) was a later programme which helped the user to uncover the themes and variations with respect to their problems. A central component of this latter programme was the Repertory Grid discussed by Kelly, and it is this which helped comprehension of the classifications people construct around their experiences and, if required, to reconstruct views on a problem. A growth in interest in the development of computer programs to aid creative-thinking problem solving took place in the 1980s.

While the above programmes assisted in making the users more aware of their own thought processes, none facilitated the restructuring of the user's thinking in order to provide a basis for creative thought. The fact that people understand their thought processes and can organise them in a systematic way is not always a sufficient condition to encourage the generation of creative insights. Kelly (1955) had argued that it was first necessary to go through the process of destructuring existing thought patterns before one could hope to gain any insights into a problem.

Some of the programmes developed in the 1980s attempted to introduce mechanisms that would help people to destructure and restructure their thinking. Brainstormer, for example, was such a programme and, using the morphological approach, divided a problem along major dimensions or themes. It presented a structured approach to creative problem solving and facilitated three-dimensional morphological analysis. Creators of computer-assisted creative problem solving aids adopted different approaches. One such approach was reflected in the Idea Generator. The programme encouraged the user to employ a fairly wide range of analogical reasoning methods. Methods included asking the user to relate similar situations to the problem, thinking up metaphors for the situation, and developing other perspectives. The programme also included sections which helped people focus on goals and on the reverse of goals. In addition, there was a section which helped the user to evaluate ideas.

Several of these early programmes attempted to take people through a number of stages of the creative problem solving process, while others made specific use of the computer's ability to randomise events or help in recording and restructuring ideas. Some of the programmes facilitated more than one of these features. In very recent times the advent of tablet computers and growth of interest in writing apps for these machines has led to cheap programmes becoming available that will perform a number of the techniques covered in this book.

Purpose-built creative solving programmes are not the only way of stimulating creative thinking with the aid of a computer. There are other ways in which computers can assist in this process. Let us look at some of the recent trends that have taken place.

The World Wide Web

Worldwide communications, including the internet, are good ways to bring people together for sharing ideas. Internet access offers facilities for bringing people together in a virtual meeting room and aids the generation of ideas and discussion. Meeting-room technology transforms the way people meet, improving the performance of people and the organisation. It can be used for brainstorming, problem solving, team building, strategic planning, and interactive learning.

Electronic brainstorming is argued to be a better technique than verbal brainstorming (Dennis and Valacich, 1994). The technique permits one to take advantage of working by oneself, thereby reducing the risk of blocking, but at the same time has the advantage of benefiting from inputs of the other group members. It is also maintained that the novelty of technology appears to make up for the cognitive inertia that characterises informative overload in the productivity of groups.

The growth of internet social network groups such as on Facebook and Twitter has led to a new way of creating and sharing ideas. One can work with a circle of friends or associates based at any place on Earth where one can get internet access. Formal idea-generating with other members of the group or simply exchanging views or advice can lead to insights into problems in hand.

Twitter offers not only the opportunity for interactions with one's group of friends or associates, it also enables one to followed pick up ideas from various corporate organisations and media creators such as *The Guardian* and *The Economist*. Regular tweaks of interface can be followed. Potentially, Twitter is a useful tool to make use of when it comes to getting and sharing ideas. Just by reading others' tweets one can set off creative lines of thought. Marketers are interested in getting ideas about trends and topics of interest that they can use to their advantage in promoting their goods and services. Social networks such as Twitter, Facebook, and the professional network LinkedIn are excellent sources from which this kind of information can be gleaned simply by reading and taking in comments and material placed on these websites.

However, it is by being proactive oneself that one can get specific ideas about a subject of interest. In this instance, it is not sufficient to just put out a question on Twitter. One should put it to a specific group of people or use popular hash tags to increase the question's exposure. This means it is important to have built up a well-defined set of people with whom one interacts on a fairly regular basis on Twitter. Another useful approach is to look for tweets which include a keyword/topic of interest along with a question mark (e.g. creativity?). This can make it possible to get a sense of how much other people may be interested in the topic. One can try to start tweeting with them about common interests (Brown, 2011).

Crowdsourcing

This might take the form of a web-based business model that solicits the creative insights into problems offered by a distributed network of individuals on the internet. It would do this by openly inviting suggestions. It would involve outsourcing a task usually carried out by employees of a company to an unknown substantial network of people. Usually, a firm might post a problem online to which a large number of individuals offer solutions. The suggestion which is judged most useful would then be rewarded and the company would make use of the idea. Facebook, too, is seen by some businesses as a medium to use for crowdsourcing.

Blogs and everyday activities

Creativity has started penetrating into everyday activities people due to the vast growth of the internet. Let's take an example of a person cooking a recipe and posting it on his or her blog. Thousands of other users looking for a similar recipe come across it and attempt new variations with the same recipe and post this recipe on the same blog. This in turn stimulates others and this cycle goes on in an infinite loop. The same thing happens in every field and topic in our everyday life. Thus, the internet and computers have made our lives more creative.

Visual analogy

The internet has many image files which can be easily accessed with a search engine such as Google. One can also use one's own photographs to stimulate creative thinking in a number of different ways. One possible way is as discussed below.

One can keep a stock of unusual photographs on a computer. The photographs can be of real events. Alternatively, given modern technological help that can be provided by photograph-manipulating programmes they can be 'manufactured' to give special effects. Such photographs can be used as visual stimuli in the use of visual analogies to get insight into problems. The first step is to select a suitable photograph as an analogy for the problem. Next, one needs to create a problem associated with the picture. Visual images that one can take with one's own camera can readily be manipulated with available software to present distorted, exaggerated, or unusual images.

There are many ways in which one might use photographs as visual stimuli and create different techniques of your own.

Databases

A firm's internal records can be scanned to help solve customers' problems. In addition, external databases can be searched for information which has an influence on pending organisational decisions. Essentially databases are storage facilities for data, information, and, most importantly, for knowledge. Existing information in computerised databases can be examined, reassessed, and made use of so that it becomes new *explicit* knowledge. Such knowledge can then be put to good use in solving new problems that may arise. For example, many large companies examine point-of-sales data to discover not only what does and does not sell, but also to find new ways to expanding their sales. The data held reflects the type of outlets where the sales have been made and the profiles of the customers using those stores. This enables the firm to identify characteristics of the shoppers at different stores and what they actually buy. Changes in patterns can readily be recognised and adjustments then made to marketing tactics to enable suitable merchandise to be supplied and apt future sales promotions.

Perhaps even more sophisticated is the use of databases for turning *explicit* knowledge into *tacit* knowledge. The latter reflects experience that has been gained by individuals and which would be beneficial to the organisation if it could be shared and accessed by all members of the organisation. For example, customer complaints could be entered into a database and other members interacting with customers could then use the knowledge it creates to experience for themselves the kinds of things about which complaints have been raised. The search facility on a database can readily list material on the insertion of a keyword.

Visualisation

Data visualisation can stimulate creativity in problem solving. It limits the scope of information search facilitating visual detection of patterns in data representations, allowing exploration and filtering of information and continuous discovery of new information. It permits us to make sense of the analysed data, turning it into new knowledge and gaining creative insights. The main purpose of visualisation is to enable us to experience data in new ways, and thus appeal to their intuition (Cybulski*et al,* 2015).

Maps

A good example of visualisation put into practice is to be found in the creation and use of maps. There are printed maps and digitised maps and both are examples of the power of visualisation. Google maps is an example of a digitised map which can also provide much more information than just roads and routes in an area. The location of many different types of businesses along with ancillary information obtained through links to their websites can be summoned at the touch of button. Such maps also provide routing information between different points showing distances and estimating times to travel on foot as well as by other means. Linked to these we also find 'street views' enabling us to undertake simulated travel along routes and actually see the premises at the roadside as we pass by. There are also digital maps which show the position of aircraft travelling the world, giving details of their actual progress in real time and of their place of origin, destination, and expected arrival time. These digital maps also show aircraft speed and altitude. Similarly, there are digital maps which show similar data regarding ships throughout the world. On a lesser scale one can also obtain apps on one's computer or phone that show where all the London tube trains are at any one time.

Objects and layouts

Other examples involve the use of three-dimensional representations of objects which can be created directly by digital means. These enable one to adjust the layout of the objects involved. One can create virtual living spaces where one can exercise creativity and imagination to produce the most pleasing effects.

Simulation

Simulation goes hand in hand with visualisation and involves a wide range of situations, from flying jet airliners to docking cruise liners. In these situations, one can learn how to deal safely with emergency situations and how to use machines in risk-free situations.

Strategy

Eppler *et al.* (2006.) also propose a framework for visualisation in the strategy process, and provide examples of typical visual formats that may be used within this framework. For example, one of the elements within the framework involves elaborating on information, discovering new patterns, building a common understanding, and developing options. In this connection they note that decision trees, concept maps, mind maps, and influence diagrams among other aids are useful.

Concept maps

Concept maps comprise linked nodes labelled with descriptive text. The text should contain a word or short phrase representing the concept and similarly labelled links between the concepts. Concept maps facilitate visualising the connections between ideas and arranging them in a logical structure (see Figure 10.1).

Artificial Intelligence

Computational models of creativity have featured in research into creativity. Using Artificial Intelligence to simulate creativity is an emerging and developing area and Mekwen *et al.* (2019) reviewed the recent computational models of aspects of human creativity. Such models allow for a mechanistic approach to cognitive processes. One recent development of this has involved experimenting with computational models using knowledge of

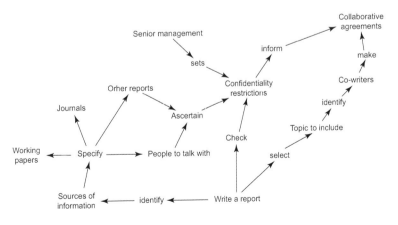

Figure 10.1 Concept map

how humans perform creative problem solving. Olteţeanu (2020) has developed a framework to examine whether a diverse set of creative problem solving tasks can be solved computationally using a unified set of principles. She described the implementation of prototype Artificial Intelligence systems, and the experiments conducted with them (see also Bahety and Olteteanu, 2019).

Artificial Intelligence and Big Data

Artificial Intelligence (AI) is used in a variety of other ways and can be found across a large number of sectors, from assembly-line robots to advanced toys, and from speech-recognition systems to medical research. Its most common application is to find patterns in data, which is why it is commonly applied in online search engines and recommendation sites.

AI can allow users of Big Data to automate and enhance complex descriptive and predictive analytical tasks that would be extremely labour intensive and time consuming if performed by hand. An instance is Google Translate which is said to incorporate billions of pages of translations into its judgement.

At the simplest level, search engines such a Google can assist users with problem by finding answers or insights which although not known to the user may already have been uncovered by other users. Web search engines vary in the way they operate but all search the Web – or select pieces of the Web – based on important words. They keep an index of the words they find, and where they find them. They allow users to look for words or combinations of words found in that index (Franklin, 2010). Of course, if the problem and solution to it have not been reported on the Web, then it is necessary to consider a different approach.

Questions

1   What do you consider to be the essentials of a creative problem solving programme? Do you think it should provide a structured approach to the whole CPS process or should it just concentrate on one aspect of it?
2   Design a creative problem solving programme which you think could help people to deal with different kinds of open-ended problem.
3   How do you visualise computer-assisted creative problem solving developing in the future?
4   Do you think crowdsourcing is a good idea? Why, or why not?
5   Suggest how you might use Facebook and Twitter to get insights you may want into a pressing problem.

6 How might AI and Big Data be harnessed to aid creative thinking and problem solving?

7 How might visualisation lead to creative insights?

8 Will Artificial Intelligence ever be able to undertake creative problem solving? Discuss.

References

Bahety, A. and Olteteanu, A. (2019) 'Approach to computational creation of insight problems using CreaCogs principles', Cognitive Systems Group, Human-Centered Computing, Freie Universitat Berlin, Germany ana-maria.olteteanu@ fu-berlin.de.

Brown, M. (2011) 'Brain zooming, 7 Ideas for using Twitter to be more creative', 23rd June, available at http://brainzooming.com/7-ways-twitter-boosts-creative-ideas-beats-creative-blocks/8132/, accessed 14 January 2013.

Cybulski, J.L. Keller, S., Nguyen, L. and Saundage, D. (2015) 'Creative problem solving in digital space using visual analytics', *Computers in Human Behavior*, 42, 20–35.

Dennis, A.R. and Valacich, J.S. (1994) 'Group, sub-group, and nominal group idea generation: new rules for a new media?', *Journal of Management*, 4, 723–36.

Eppler, M.J., Platts, K. and Kazancioglu, E. (2006) 'Visual strategizing: the systematic use of visualization in the strategy process', Universita della Svizzera italiana, Faculty of Communication Sciences, Institute for Corporate Communication, Paper #7/2006, December, available at http://rero.ch/record /6186/files/wpca0607.pdf, accessed 18 April 2013.

Franklin, C. (2010) 'How Internet search engines work', howstufworks, available at http://www.howstuffworks.com/search-engine.htm, accessed 11.1.2010.

Kelly, G.A. (1955) *The Psychology of Personal Constructs*, New York: Norton.

Mekern, V., Hommel, B. and Sjoerds, Z. (2019) 'Computational models of creativity: a review of single- process and multi-process recent approaches to demystify creative cognition', *Current Opinion in Behavioral Sciences*, 27, 47–54.

Olteţeanu, A. (2020) *Cognition and the Creative Machine: Cognitive AI for Creative Problem Solving*, Springer.

Rokeach, M. (1979) *Understanding Human Values: Individual and Societal*, New York: Free Press.

Shaw, M.L. (1982) 'PLANET: some experience in creating an integrated system for repertory grid applications on a microcomputer', *International Journal of Man-Machine Studies*, 17, 345–60.

Simon, H.A. (1985) 'What we know about the creative process', in R.L. Kuhn (ed.), *Frontiers in Creative and Innovative Management*, New York: Ballinger, 3–22.

Further reading

Brabham, D.C. (2013) *Crowdsourcing*, Cambridge: MIT Press.

Hussain, M. and Jatinder, M. (2016) 'Artificial intelligence for big data: potential and relevance', *International Academy of Engineering and Medical Research*, 1(1), 1–5.

Indurkhya, B. (2013) 'Computers and creativity', in Veale, T., Feyaerts, K. and Forceville, C.J. (eds), *Creativity and the Agile Mind*, Berlin: De Gruyter Mouton, 61–79.

Proctor, T. (1993) 'Computer stimulated associations', *Creativity Research Journal*, 6(4), 391–400.

Index

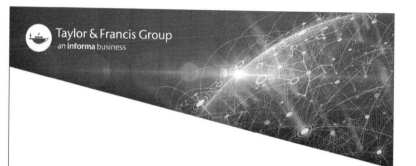

Printed in the United States
by Baker & Taylor Publisher Services